PUBLICATIONS

OF THE

SCOTTISH HISTORY SOCIETY

THIRD SERIES
VOLUME
XLIII

———◆———

SCOTTISH POPULATION STATISTICS

including

WEBSTER'S ANALYSIS OF POPULATION 1755

1952   A

THE REV. ALEXANDER WEBSTER, D.D.

SCOTTISH POPULATION STATISTICS

including

WEBSTER'S ANALYSIS OF POPULATION 1755

Edited by

JAMES GRAY KYD

C.B.E., F.R.S.E., F.F.A.

EDINBURGH

Printed by T. and A. Constable Ltd.
Printers to the University of Edinburgh
for the Scottish History Society

1952

Printed in Great Britain

CONTENTS

A generous contribution from the Carnegie Trust for the Universities of Scotland towards the cost of producing this volume is gratefully acknowledged by the Council of the Society.

FOREWORD

THE primary object of this volume is to publish Webster's Census of 1755, of which the original manuscript is in the National Library of Scotland.

In order, however, to give a background against which Webster's enumeration may be viewed, some information is given both on the attempts which were made to estimate the population of Scotland before 1755 and on the official Censuses which were initiated at the beginning of the nineteenth century.

JAMES GRAY KYD.

EDINBURGH, 1951.

INTRODUCTION

IT is a difficult task to estimate the number of inhabitants of a country by any means other than a census, and without a census to gauge their age structure or their distribution—topographical and occupational—is almost impossible.

The first official census was taken in modern Britain in the year 1801, and it is from this date that reliable facts are available in regard to the population. From 1801 there was a census every ten years till 1931 ; and a National Register of the civilian population was taken in 1939. Owing to the War there was no census in 1941, but one was taken in 1951. The information obtained at the various censuses has not always been the same. The number of persons of each sex has been obtained at every census, but the ages of the people were obtained for the first time in 1821, and again in 1841, and thereafter at every subsequent enumeration. Marital condition was first included in the census of 1851 and has appeared at each census since then. Questions relating to fertility were asked in the census of 1911, and again in 1951.

Scotland made demographic history when Webster took his census in 1755 which, if not the earliest European census taken since the days of the Roman Empire, is one of the very earliest. A census appears to have been taken in England and Wales in 1695, but the results were never published ; a census was also taken in Sweden in 1749 and one in Austria the year before Webster made his enumeration, but before describing Webster's census it would be well to give some information as to the attempts which were made to estimate the population of these islands as it was before the national censuses were inaugurated.

Official estimates of population seem to have been made

much more frequently in regard to the population of
England and Wales than they were for the Scottish population. In fact, estimating population seems to have been
a popular pastime south of the Border. In the reports on
the censuses both of 1831 and 1841 estimates were given
which have the imprimatur of official accuracy. For the
1831 Census Volume, Finlaison, the actuary to the National
Debt Commissioners, was consulted and he gave the
following estimates [1] of the population of England and
Wales at decennial points throughout the eighteenth
century [1] :—

	Thousands
1700	5135
1710	5066
1720	5345
1730	5688
1740	5830
1750	6040
1760	6480
1770	7228
1780	7815
1790	8541
1800	9187

The 1841 volume contains the result of an attempt by
John Rickman (the officer in charge of the census) to
estimate the population of England and Wales at various
dates from 1570 to 1750. The method adopted by him
was to assume that the average number of baptisms,
burials and marriages recorded in the local parish registers
in the three years around each of the dates 1570, 1600, 1630,
1670, 1700 and 1750 (which the local Clergy extracted for
him from their registers) bore the same relation to the

---

[1] 1831 Census report, Volume I, Preface, page xlv.

actual population at these respective dates as the corresponding average did to the population in the year 1801, which was known from the census enumeration. The figures for the total population of England and Wales at these various dates were thus estimated as follows :—

	Thousands
1570	4160
1600	4811
1630	5600
1670	5774
1700	6045
1750	6517
1801	8873

Rickman died in 1840, but the result of his work was published posthumously in the 1841 census volume.[1] The divergence between the two official estimates at common points of time casts doubt on the accuracy of either.

Black, in his historic treatise " on Mortality of the Human Species," [2] published in 1788, was well aware of the wide margin of error in all these early population estimates. In his own words he states, " But if in London alone, where registers of various kinds may be consulted, calculators are, notwithstanding, at variance respecting its population upwards of one hundred thousand and in the whole island more than a million—as well might we expect a list of the lions, crocodiles, and monkeys of Africa as of the outcast human race in those burning and illiterate regions."

The habit of estimating the size of the population, however, was not entirely confined to England and Wales.

---

[1] Census 1841, Part I, p. 36.

[2] *A Comparative View of Mortality of the Human Species at all Ages*, by William Black, M.S. (Published at the unanimous request of the Medical Society of London. Printed for C. Dilly in the Poultry—1788.)

Templeman in 1729 in his *New Survey of the Globe*,[1] gave estimates of " the numbers of people in all ye principal Countries and Cities of Europe calculated from the number of houses or bills of mortality." He estimated the population of Scotland at that time at 1,500,000.

A well-known Scottish divine, the Rev. Dr. Robert Wallace—the man who carried out the calculation for Webster's Ministers' Widows' Fund—wrote " A Dissertation on the Number of Mankind",[2] in which he indicates that in his opinion Templeman's estimate of 1,500,000 was too high for the population of Scotland. David Hume also embarked on this perilous sea of guesswork in his political discourse entitled " On the Populousness of Civilised Nations," and apparently an attempt was also made by Sir Robert Sibbald about 1680 to enumerate the people of Scotland, but his project was never accomplished.[3] From an examination of Sibbald's work it would seem that his conception was more of the nature of Sinclair's *Statistical Account of Scotland* than on the lines of a census.

In addition to *ad hoc* enumerations made for census purposes, certain limited information regarding population can be obtained from Poll Tax Returns of 1694-95, Hearth Tax Rolls of 1683-84 and the Seaforth Papers dated 1797. Further details in regard to these are included in Appendix III.

But all these attempts were little more than educated guesses, and it was not until Webster took his census of 1755 that we are able to leave the realms of fancy for the sure facts of enumeration.

---

[1] *A New Survey of the Globe*, by Thomas Templeman of St. Edmunds Bury, Suffolk. Engraved by Cole in Great King Street in Hatton Gardens, London—1729.

[2] *A Dissertation on the Number of Mankind in Ancient and Modern Times*, p. 88. Printed for G. Hamilton by J. Balfour (Edinburgh, 1753).

[3] *Dictionary of National Biography, sub voc.* Sibbald.

Webster was born in 1707 and was elected Moderator of the General Assembly of the Church of Scotland in 1753. He was a popular preacher as minister of the Tolbooth Church, Edinburgh, and, as one of the city functionaries observed, " it was easier to get a seat in the Kingdom of Heaven than in the Tolbooth Kirk." He held many offices in the Church. He was a chaplain in ordinary to His Majesty and in his old age, when his way of life rendered him unsuited to act as pastor of the Tolbooth Church, he became administrator of the Widows' Fund which he himself had initiated.

Opinions vary as to the man, but all agree that he was one who lived well. His fondness for claret brought him the nickname of Dr. Bonum Magnum. The Rev. Alexander Carlyle of Inveresk, who was closely associated with him, writes, " Though Webster was a clever fellow, an excellent and ready speaker, fertile in expedient, and prompt in execution, yet he had by no means a leading and decisive mind." [1]

Webster seems to have been a man of outstanding personality. He made his reputation largely from the fact that his name was closely associated with the initiation of the Fund for the Widows and Orphans of the Ministers of the Church of Scotland. In actual fact there is no doubt that the actuarial basis of the scheme was largely the work of a colleague of Webster's, the Rev. Dr. Robert Wallace, who also appears to have been deeply interested in the mathematics of population, as is evidenced by the publication of his *Dissertation on the Number of Mankind*. Webster, however, seems to have been the leading spirit in the inauguration of the Fund, and when the Rev. Dr. Price, the famous English actuary, in the first edition of his work on

[1] *Autobiography of Dr. Alexander Carlyle,* 3rd edition, p. 238 (Wm. Blackwood & Sons).

annuities,[1] challenged the soundness of Webster's scheme, the ink was barely dry on Price's treatise before Webster wrote a letter of some 4500 words to Price explaining the basis of his plan. This letter was dated Edinburgh, 4th October 1771, and Dr. Price's reply, which was a complete withdrawal of all criticism, was dated London, 21st of the same month. In view of the time taken in the conveyance of mails from Edinburgh to London in those days, Dr. Price's complete vindication of the Scottish scheme was evidently considered by him to be a matter of extreme urgency. The correspondence was published in full by Murray and Cochran of Edinburgh in 1771. Dr. Price's criticism does not appear in any of the many subsequent editions of his work on annuities.

Although Webster had no scruples and seemed to be entirely without principles, his establishment of the Widows' Fund gained for him much respect among the clergy. His appearance of great strictness in religion did not act in restraint of his convivial humour. He could pass instantly from the most unbounded jollity to the most fervent devotion. In Boswell's *Journal of a Tour to the Hebrides*, it is stated of a visit to Edinburgh—" At supper we had Dr. Alexander Webster who, though not learned, had such a knowledge of mankind and a fund of information and entertainment, so clear a head and such accommodating manners that Dr. Johnson found him a very agreeable companion." [2]

Notwithstanding all his human frailties Webster was a great ecclesiastical leader, and his name will long be remembered in Church circles by virtue of his work on the Ministers' Widows' Fund and among demographers as the

---

[1] *Observations on Reversionary Payment*, by Richard Price, D.D., F.R.S. London—Printed for T. Cadell in the Strand—1771.

[2] *Journal of a Tour to the Hebrides with Samuel Johnson, LL.D.*, p. 32 Isham Collection, William Heinemann, London, 1930).

author of the first census ever taken in Britain in modern days.

The method employed by Webster for enumerating the people is fully explained in his own words in his introduction, which is printed in this volume. It may be pointed out that he was in a particularly favoured position to induce the ministers to comply with the request to count their parishioners. In the first place he was acting on behalf of the Government, for it would appear that Lord President Dundas at the instigation of the Government commissioned Webster to obtain figures as to the population of Scotland; secondly, he was Moderator of the General Assembly of the Church of Scotland; and, thirdly, his name was closely associated with the preparation of the scheme for the provision of annuities for the widows and children of the clergy.

The plan he adopted for his census was to induce the Society for the Propagation of Christian Knowledge in the Highlands and Islands to require every minister in those Presbyteries where the Society had erected Charity Schools, to enumerate his parishioners, and in default the minister was informed that the Society would withdraw the schools. In districts where the Society was not represented Webster sent a schedule of queries to the parish minister, and the eminence of his position in the Church and the fact that he was acting on behalf of the State ensured that compliance with the request was speedy and accurate.

Webster's census enumeration is printed in its entirety on pages 1-81. It will be observed that according to him the total population of Scotland in 1755 was 1,265,380. From page x it will be seen that two estimates of the population of England and Wales are available at the mid-point of the eighteenth century. The arithmetic mean of these estimates gives a population of 6,278,000.

Lord Cooper, in his article, "The Number and Distribution of the Population of Mediaeval Scotland," in *The
Scottish Historical Review*,[1] expressed the opinion that before
the nineteenth century, when the population south of the
Border began to increase more rapidly than that of Scotland, the population of England and Wales may be taken
to be about five times that of Scotland. It is worthy of
note that the population of Scotland as found by Webster
is almost exactly one-fifth of the mean of the estimated
population of England and Wales in 1750. This seems to
confirm Lord Cooper's view on the relative size of the
population in the two parts of Great Britain in the static
period which preceded the great expansion of the nineteenth
century.

Before the days when Scotland had a Registrar-General
the population censuses were controlled from London. In
England and Wales the census returns were supervised
locally by the Overseers of the Poor. The following
quotation from the preface to the report on the 1831
census indicates how the work was undertaken on this side
of the Border : " In Scotland the machinery for the execution of the Population Act has been usually deemed more
perfect there than in England, inasmuch as it is committed
to the care of the official Schoolmasters of each parish, an
institution peculiar to Scotland which has existed in full
vigour since the year 1696. (The ' teachers of youth ' were
in Scotland recognised and placed under regulation by
statute A.D. 1567 and Parochial Schools were established
by law in Scotland A.D. 1696.) And as the office of Pre-
centor and Clerk to the Parochial Session for poor relief
is often combined with that of Schoolmaster the personal
knowledge of the number of children in every parish
appertains to the Schoolmasters in Scotland as to the

---

[1] *Scottish Historical Review*, XXVI, pp. 2-9.

Overseers in England, and the habit of regularity together
with the official knowledge of writing and arithmetic
implied in the character of the Schoolmaster renders the
population return in Scotland quite as authentic and
obviously more methodical than those received from the
Overseers of the poor in England."

From Webster's total of 1,265,000 the population grew
to 1,608,000 in 1801, and as shown below the population
increased at each subsequent census until that of 1921,
but the effect of the net loss of nearly 400,000 Scots by
emigration in the decennium 1921-31 resulted in the
population of Scotland in 1931 being some 40,000 less than
that of ten years earlier.

POPULATION OF SCOTLAND AT EACH CENSUS

	Males	Females	Both Sexes	Inter-censal Increase	Rate of Increase Per cent.	Ratio of Females to each 100 Males
1801	739091	869329	1608420	—		117·6
1811	826296	979568	1805864	197444	12·3	118·5
1821	982623	1108898	2091521	285657	15·8	112·9
1831	1114456	1249930	2364386	272865	13·0	112·2
1841	1241862	1378322	2620184	255798	10·8	111·0
1851	1375479	1513263	2888742	268558	10·2	110·0
1861	1449848	1612446	3062294	173552	6·0	111·2
1871	1603143	1756875	3360018	297724	9·7	109·6
1881	1799475	1936098	3735573	375555	11·2	107·6
1891	1942717	2082930	4025647	290074	7·8	107·2
1901	2173755	2298348	4472103	446456	11·1	105·7
1911	2308839	2452065	4760904	288801	6·5	106·2
1921	2347642	2534855	4882497	121593	2·6	108·0
1931	2325523	2517457	4842980	−39517	−0·8	108·3
1951 (20 years)	2434749	2661220	5095969	252989	5·2	109·3

While the population has grown more than threefold
between 1801 and 1951 the intercensal increases have
fallen rapidly during the present century. The distribution

B

of the population according to age, area and occupation has altered very greatly. As indicated on page ix the ages of the people were not taken at the earlier censuses and the same applies to the question of occupation, but definite facts are known in regard to the topographical distribution of the population right back to the census of 1755.

If we divide Scotland into three areas representing roughly the Highlands, the Lowlands and the narrow Central Belt which lies between, we get the following distribution in 1755, in 1861 and at the date of the last census in 1951.

(The Central Belt comprises the Counties of Ayr, Dunbarton, Lanark, Renfrew, Clackmannan, Stirling, the Lothians, Fife and the City of Dundee. The Highland area is that lying north of the Central Belt and the Lowlands are that lying south of it.)

District	Size of area in square miles	Fraction of Total	Popn. in Thous.	% of Total	Density persons per square mile
			1755		
Highland	21330	5/7	652	51	31
Central	4269	1/7	464	37	110
Lowland	4196	1/7	149	11	36
	29795		1265		42
			1861		
Highland	21330	5/7	1020	33	48
Central	4269	1/7	1769	58	414
Lowland	4196	1/7	273	9	65
	29795		3062		103
			1951		
Highland	21330	5/7	1000	20	47
Central	4269	1/7	3840	75	900
Lowland	4196	1/7	256	5	61
	29795		5096		171

It will be seen that in the middle of the eighteenth century more than half of the population lived north of the Central Belt, but by 1951 only one-fifth of the population were in this district, which constitutes more than 70 per cent. of the area of Scotland. More dramatic still, however, is the fact that by 1951 three-quarters of the population were concentrated with a density of 900 persons to the square mile into the Central Belt, which comprises but one-seventh of the area of Scotland. These figures indicate the profound changes which have taken place since the middle of the eighteenth century in the regional distribution of our population.

The growth of population depends normally on the excess of births over deaths—commonly called the " natural increase." In modern times with the improved facilities for travel and with the opening up of new fields of development throughout the world the growth in a population may be greatly affected by migration.

The birth-rate has been falling since the last decade of the nineteenth century, and although the death-rate began to fall about the same time its fall has not been so rapid. Consequently the rate of natural increase of the population has had a downward trend for about sixty years.

The further decremental force of emigration has markedly affected our population growth. The following table gives quinquennial averages for birth, death and natural increase rates to 1940. As the rates for years after 1940 were violently affected by war conditions, they are given for individual years. The migration rates are shown in decennial averages up to 1931.

TABLE I

Quinquennial averages of rates of birth, death and natural increase from 1855-60 to 1936-40 and individual yearly rates from 1941 to 1950. Rates of migration loss for each decennium from 1861 to 1931 with rate for the twenty year period 1931-51.

Period	Rates of			Annual Loss by migration per 1000 of Earlier Census Population
	Birth	Death	Natural Increase	
1855–60	34·1	20·8	13·3	
1861–65	35·1	22·1	13·0	3·8
1866–70	34·9	22·0	12·9	
1871–75	35·0	22·7	12·3	2·8
1876–80	34·8	20·6	14·2	
1881–85	33·3	19·6	13·7	5·8
1886–90	31·4	18·8	12·6	
1891–95	30·5	19·0	11·5	1·3
1896–00	30·0	17·9	12·1	
1901–05	29·2	17·1	12·1	5·7
1906–10	27·6	16·1	11·5	
1911–15	25·4	15·7	9·7	5·0
1916–20	22·8	15·0	7·8	
1921–25	23·0	13·9	9·1	8·0
1926–30	20·0	13·6	6·4	
1931–35	18·2	13·2	5·0	
1936–40	17·6	13·5	4·1	
1941	17·5	14·7	2·8	
1942	17·6	13·3	4·3	
1943	18·4	14·0	4·4	
1944	18·5	13·6	4·9	4·5
1945	16·9	13·2	3·7	
1946	20·3	13·1	7·2	
1947	22·0	12·9	9·1	
1948	19·4	11·8	7·6	
1949	18·5	12·3	6·2	
1950	17·9	12·4	5·5	

In Plate A on page xxxiv these rates are displayed in graphic form. It will be seen that in the third decade of this century the emigration rate exceeded the rate of natural increase ; consequently the population fell.

The following Table II shows for each population census since 1871 the actual natural increase, the intercensal increase and the net loss by migration.

TABLE II

Period	Natural Increase	Intercensal Increase in Population	Net Migration Loss
1861–1871	414726	297724	117002
1871–1881	468883	375555	93328
1881–1891	507492	290074	217418
1891–1901	499812	446456	53356
1901–1911	542843	288801	254042
1911–1921	360180	121593	238587
1921–1931	352386	–39517	391903
1931–1951	502293	252989	220000

It will be observed that for every intercensal period up to 1931 the increase (or decrease) in population is represented by the natural increase *less* the net migration loss. In the twenty years ending 1951, however, this relationship does not hold. It is understood that this apparent discrepancy is related to the number of Scots in the armed forces temporarily away from Scotland on the census date in 1951. While the loss by migration in the latter half of the nineteenth century was great, giving a decrement averaging about 3 per cent. of the population, it was not until the dawn of the twentieth century that the continuous high level flow of migrants commenced.

From 1901 to 1931 the net loss by migration was approximately 885,000, and for the first half of this century this loss has exceeded 1,100,000.

While the rate of loss between the census of 1931 and that of 1951 is at the lowest level of this century it must be recollected that in the early thirties large numbers of Scots returned to the homeland from the other side of the Atlantic owing to industrial depression abroad, and during the years of the 1939-45 war, not only was overseas emigration entirely prohibited but large numbers returned to Scotland to help in the war effort at home.

It would appear that from 1931 up to the end of hostilities in 1945 Scotland gained by migration and that the loss of some 220,000 has occurred in the six years preceding the census date in 1951. This fact would seem to indicate a much more serious drain on the Scottish population than is represented by a loss of 220,000 in twenty years.

No country on the continent of Europe has lost such a high proportion of her people as Scotland, and if comparison is made between Scottish losses and those of England and Wales the great exodus of the Scots is apparent from the following startling figures :—

TABLE III

Years	Net Loss by Migration			
	England and Wales	Percentage of Population	Scotland	Percentage of Population
1901–1911	501000	1·5	254000	5·7
1911–1921	620000	1·7	239000	5·0
1921–1931	172000	0·5	392000	8·0
1931–1951	745000 (Gain)	1·8	220000	4·5

In each of the decennial periods up to 1931 Scotland's rate of loss is much greater than that of England and Wales, but her loss reached a climax in the ten years 1921-31 when it was sixteen times that south of the Border. In actual numbers the loss in England and Wales was less than half that of Scotland, notwithstanding the fact that their population is eight times that of Scotland.

It is a significant fact, as is shown in the above table, that while England and Wales gained by migration nearly three-quarters of a million between the census of 1931 and that of 1951, Scotland lost 220,000 in the same period.

It is too early yet after the Second World War to form any definite view as to the future migration position in Scotland, but there are indications that the countries of the British Commonwealth are ready and anxious to welcome well-trained young Scots of both sexes, and the alarming rate of loss in the immediate post-war period before 1951 would seem to indicate that migration will be an important factor in Scotland's demographic history for many years to come.

The high rate of migration from Scotland compared with that of England and Wales is reflected in the relative growth of the population in the two countries. The following Table IV shows the populations of both countries at the beginning and half-way through both the nineteenth and the twentieth centuries.

TABLE IV

| Year | England and Wales | | Scotland | | Scottish Population expressed as a percentage of that of England and Wales |
	Population in thousands	Proportion of 1801 Population	Population in thousands	Proportion of 1801 Population	
1801	8893		1608		18·0
1851	17928	2	2889	1·8	16·2
1901	32528	3·7	4472	2·8	13·8
1951	43745	4·9	5096	3·2	11·7

It will be seen that while the population of England and Wales has increased almost five-fold in the last century and a half, the population of Scotland has slightly more than trebled in the same period. Further, it will be observed that 150 years ago Scotland's population was 18 per cent.

of that of England and Wales, whereas today it is under 12 per cent.

When it is borne in mind that the birth-rate in Scotland has exceeded that of England and Wales for fifty years and that our rate of natural increase has been the greater since 1910, the powerful effect of migration loss on Scotland's population growth is at once apparent.

As the majority of migrants are young and healthy, losses on the scale of those of this century must have a profound effect, not only on the size of our population, but on its age distribution, its economic and social vitality and on its reproductive potential.

An examination of the census figures of England and Wales, of Canada, and of the United States of America, indicates that the majority of Scots who have left their homeland have taken up their abode in one or other of these countries.

At the 1931 census of England and Wales there were 366,486 Scottish-born people living there. The Canadian census of the same year revealed that there were 279,765 people of Scottish birth in that country and the census of 1930 in the United States of America showed that there were actually 354,323 persons whose birth-place was Scotland. The majority of these people probably left Scotland in the half-century before 1930.

These figures indicate that more than a million Scottish-born people were living in one or other of these countries at the end of the third decade of this century.

It is worth recording, as a fact of history, that at the census of Canada and of the United States of America taken ten years later, during the critical early years of the 1939-45 War, the number of Scottish-born persons living in these two countries had fallen by nearly 130,000, which indicates the return of large numbers of Scots many of whom came to help in the war effort either in the home-land as civilians, or as members of the forces.

While the trend of population in Scotland as a whole has been upward, the experience of individual counties has varied greatly. Appendix I shows the population of each of our thirty-three counties at 1755 and at every official census from 1801 onwards. In order to show clearly the varying trend of the population in individual counties a table has been prepared showing the intercensal increase or decrease of each county. This is included in Appendix II and gives a broad picture of great growth in the counties of the Central Industrial Belt, of a slow increase to a maximum about the middle of the nineteenth century in the counties north of Inverness and a somewhat similar trend in the border counties which reached their maximum later than the highland counties.

The early beginnings of the industrial revolution are clearly seen by the large population increases both actual and proportional between 1755 and 1801 in the counties which are predominantly industrial.

To illustrate the diverse experience in regard to population trend in the counties the following summary, Table V, has been prepared showing the experience of three typical highland counties namely, Caithness, Sutherland and Ross and Cromarty ; three border counties, Peebles, Selkirk and Roxburgh; and three counties of the Central Industrial Belt, Lanark, Midlothian and Renfrew. Figures for Scotland as a whole are also included in the table on page xxvi.

These figures are displayed in graphic form in Plate B on page xxxv. It will be observed from an examination of Table V and the graphs that both for Scotland as a whole and in the Central industrial counties the population is at its recorded maximum in 1951 and that, apart from a slight

WEBSTER'S CENSUS

TABLE V

Population at Various Dates

Year	Three typical Highland Counties Population in hundreds	Proportion of Maximum	Three typical Border Counties Population in hundreds	Proportion of Maximum	Three typical Industrial Counties Population in hundreds	Proportion of Maximum	Scotland Population in hundreds	Proportion of maximum
1755	911	62%	476	50	1987	8	12654	25
1801	1020	69	478	50	3488	14	16084	31
1831	1348	91	611	64	6695	27	23646	36
1861	1477	100	759	79	10832	43	30623	60
1891	1369	92	959	100	17710	71	40256	79
1901	1318	89	873	91	20971	84	44721	88
1911	1296	87	871	91	22693	91	47609	92
1921	1169	79	829	86	23447	94	48825	96
1931	1046	71	835	87	23909	96	48430	95
1951	969	66	825	86	25046	100	50960	100

drop in the national population between 1921 and 1931, the trend has been steadily upward with an increasing impetus in the upward population movement of the Central Belt. The highland counties reached their maximum in 1861 and thereafter show a rapid decline to the present day when the population is practically the same as it was two hundred years earlier.

The border counties reached their maximum some thirty years later than the highland counties and their subsequent rate of decline has been less rapid.

It is worthy of note that all the four graphs show practically the same relation to their maxima at the beginning of this century, but whereas in the Central Belt and for Scotland as a whole the maximum population had not then been reached, the population in the other areas had then passed its zenith.

The decline in both the highland and border population is due to the fact that births were greatly outnumbered by the double decrement of death and migration. Actually in some areas the loss by migration exceeded the deaths.

Just as the population curve for Scotland as a whole does not give a true picture of the position in the individual counties, so the county figures by themselves—particularly in the highland area—do not necessarily reflect the true position in the parishes which make up the county. For example, in Ross and Cromarty the present population of the county as a whole has remained practically stationary during the past twenty years—it stood at 62,799 in 1931 and the census of 1951 gives the figure as 60,503.

If, however, the population trend of four typical parishes in the west of the county is compared with that of four typical parishes in the east we get the following rather startling picture.

WEBSTER'S CENSUS

TABLE VI

County of Ross and Cromarty					
Western Parishes	Population		Eastern Parishes	Population	
Name	1931	1951	Name	1931	1951
Applecross	1034	735	Dingwall	2762	3604
Glen Shiel	317	310	Rosemarkie	1203	1140
Kintail	376	297	Rosskeen	3580	3740
Lochbroom	2004	1448	Tain	2176	2350
	3731	2790		9721	10834

In the Western parishes the population has fallen by 25 per cent. in the twenty years and in the Eastern parishes the population has risen by 11 per cent. in the same period.

The same variations in the population trend of the individual parishes of the County of Sutherland is also apparent from the following table giving populations in the Western and in the South-Eastern parishes of the county. In Sutherland the population of the county as a whole has shown a decline at every census since 1851 when the maximum of 25,793 was reached. In the century

TABLE VII

County of Sutherland					
Western Parishes	Population		South-Eastern Parishes	Population	
Name	1931	1951	Name	1931	1951
Assynt	1342	889	Clyne	1723	1730
Eddrachillis	967	788	Dornoch	2086	1921
Farr	1769	1366	Golspie	1392	1323
Tongue	1184	827	Kildonan	1454	1338
	5262	3870		6655	6312

which has elapsed since that date the population has fallen to 13,664, which is little more than half the maximum figure. As will be seen from the following table, the Western parishes have suffered a more rapid decline than those in the South-East of the county.

While the population of the county as a whole fell by 15 per cent. between 1931 and 1951, in the Western parishes the fall was 26 per cent. and in the South-Eastern parishes 5 per cent.

While migration has had a pronounced influence on the growth of population in Scotland as a whole, its effect on the trend of population in the northern and southern counties has been overwhelming. Looking at the figures for the sixty years 1871 to 1931 we find the following experience in the three divisions of Scotland.

TABLE VIII

Area	Population 1871	Natural Increase	Population Growth	Net Migration Loss	Population 1931	Percentage of mean population lost by migration
Highland	1041000	519000	−61000	580000	980000	57·5
Central	2047000	2089000	1565000	524000	3612000	18·5
Lowland	272000	123000	−21000	144000	251000	55·0
Scotland	3360000	2731000	1483000	1248000	4843000	30·4

It will be observed that for Scotland as a whole the natural increase of the population exceeded the loss by migration by about one and a half millions and the population has therefore risen by this amount. In the northern and southern areas the natural increase is entirely wiped out by migration losses and the population has therefore declined. In these two parts of Scotland more than half of the mean population has been lost by migration in the sixty years.

Losses on this scale have not only reduced the numbers living in these areas ; they have also had a very pronounced effect on the age constitution of the population. In a self-contained community where the population is maintained by an excess of births over deaths, the number living in any particular age group normally exceeds the number living in each of the higher age groups of similar size. These numbers can be graphically displayed in the form of a regular pyramid. This orderly sequence is disturbed where losses by migration occur on a large scale.

In order to illustrate the effect on the age distribution of varying rates of migration, population pyramids have been prepared for

(a) Scotland as a Whole.

(b) The West-Central Counties.

(c) The Northern Counties.

These pyramids printed on pages xxxvi-xxxix show the position at 1871, before migration on the high level of later years had started, and at 1931, which marked the end of the great exodus of the early decades of the century.

Looking at the plate for Scotland as a whole it will be seen that the 1871 pyramid shows a population nourished by a steady flow of births but subject to a high rate of infant mortality.

The 1931 pyramid reveals clearly the following facts :—

(1) The losses of men in the 1914-18 War, and by migration. These are apparent from the depression in the numbers of males in the age groups 30-50. The depression in the number of women in this age group is much less than that among

men as migration alone was the decremental force
other than normal mortality.

(2) The reduced birth-rate during the war years is
evidenced by the unnaturally small number of each
sex living in the age group 10-15.

(3) The boom in births in the immediate post-war
years of 1920-21 is shown by the large number
living in the age group 5-10.

(4) The fall in the birth-rate after the post-war boom
is evident by the fact that the numbers living in
the first quinquennium of life is less than the
number in the age group 5-10.

(5) The increased proportion of the population living
at ages over sixty compared with the earlier date
is due to the extension of the average duration of
human life.

The pyramids for the West Central area closely resemble
those for Scotland as a whole. This is natural as a large
proportion of the population of Scotland lives in this area.
There are, however, differences. The South-Western area
nearly doubled its population in the sixty years, and at
the later date the proportion of the population living at
the productive ages is markedly greater than in Scotland
as a whole. This excess must be due to the high birth-rate
in the area and to the immigration of young people from
other parts of Scotland.

The pyramids for the Northern Counties show an entirely
different picture from the other two areas.

It will be observed that even in 1871 the loss by migration—particularly of men—shows itself very plainly.
While the total number living in the area in 1931 is only
slightly less than in 1871, the weight of the population is

found at the older ages. The smaller proportion of the
population living in the early age groups in the 1931
pyramid is caused mainly by the falling birth-rate since
the beginning of the century.

The age distribution of these Northern counties is such
that unless some means can be found of attracting people
from outside the area, the population, particularly in the
more northerly counties, must inevitably decline very
greatly. This position is tragically true in the case of some
highland parishes where the old people now outnumber
the young and where in the ordinary course of nature the
population will dwindle until the parishes become practically uninhabited.

As an example of these conditions, population diagrams
are given for the parish of Gairloch in Wester Ross for the
years 1861 when the population was at its maximum of
5479 and for 1931 when the population had fallen to 2376.
(The preliminary report on the 1951 census shows a further
reduction to 1991.)

The 1861 pyramid shows evidence of a high birth-rate
and a fairly well-balanced population with an indication
of mass emigration in some age groups. The 1931 figure—
it can hardly be called a pyramid—shows the effect of a
falling birth-rate and a population so unbalanced in age-
grouping that there is not much variation in the numbers
living at each quinquennial age group from 0-5 to 75-80.
This maldistribution indicates that the continuance of the
normal social and economic administration of the area
must necessarily become a matter of the greatest difficulty.

In an historical treatise the main theme must relate to
the past, but the facts which have been brought out in
this volume are pointers to the future.

He would be a bold man who would dare to predict what

our population will be in the middle of the twenty-first century. Today, in 1951, it stands at about 5,100,000. Two hundred years ago it was one and a quarter millions, rising to nearly three millions at the middle of the nineteenth century. The rate of growth is slowing down. There are fewer women in the first twenty years of life than there are between 20 and 40. The birth-rate is tending to fall, and while the death-rate also has a downward trend the increasing average age of the population is bound to produce a rise. The position in regard to future migration is uncertain.

All these facts seem to indicate that, unless some great change takes place in the economic and social life of our country, a reduction in the number of our people, during the next hundred years, seems more likely than an increase.

J. G. K.

PLATE A

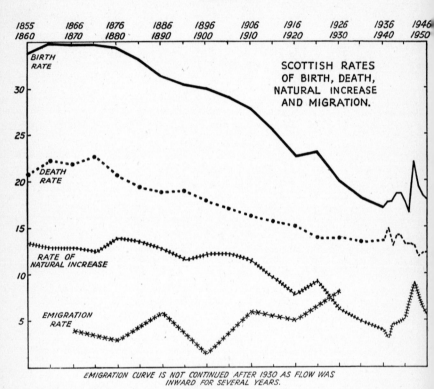

SCOTTISH RATES
OF BIRTH, DEATH,
NATURAL INCREASE
AND MIGRATION.

EMIGRATION CURVE IS NOT CONTINUED AFTER 1930 AS FLOW WAS
INWARD FOR SEVERAL YEARS.

THE ABOVE RATES ARE PER THOUSAND OF THE POPULATION.

PLATE B

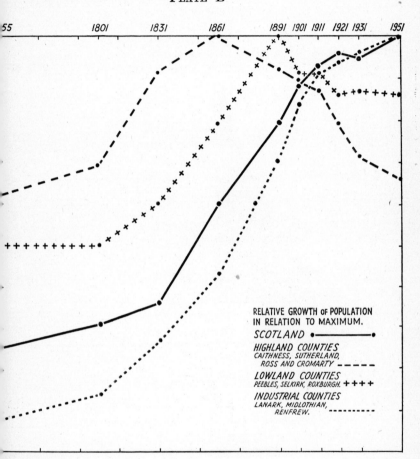

RELATIVE GROWTH OF POPULATION
IN RELATION TO MAXIMUM.
SCOTLAND •━━━━•
HIGHLAND COUNTIES
CAITHNESS, SUTHERLAND,
ROSS AND CROMARTY ━ ━ ━ ━
LOWLAND COUNTIES
PEEBLES, SELKIRK, ROXBURGH. ＋＋＋＋
INDUSTRIAL COUNTIES
LANARK, MIDLOTHIAN,
RENFREW. ----------

POPULATION OF THE WEST CENTRAL COUNTIES
OF SCOTLAND

(Reproduced from *Scottish Historical Review*, vol. xxviii.)

Dunbarton, Renfrew, Ayr, Lanark

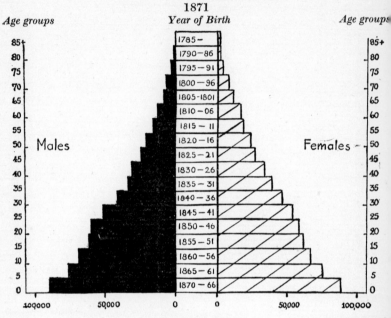

1871

Age groups | Year of Birth | Age groups

Population: 609,760 males   Total: 1,244,334   634,574 females

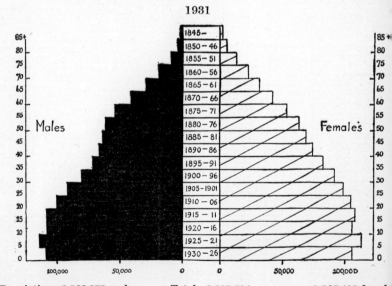

1931

Population: 1,122,171 males   Total: 2,307,594   1,185,423 females

POPULATION OF THE NORTHERN COUNTIES OF SCOTLAND

(Reproduced from *Scottish Historical Review*, vol. xxviii.)

etland, Orkney, Caithness, Sutherland, Ross and Cromarty, Inverness, Nairn, Moray,
berdeen, Banff, Kincardine, Angus (excluding Dundee), Perth, Kinross, Argyll, Bute

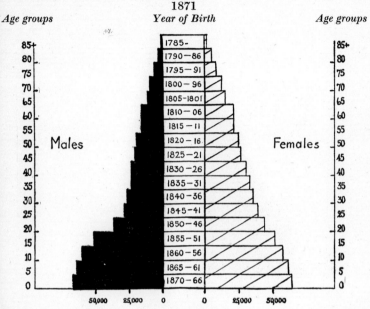

1871

pulation : 478,763 males   Total: 1,039,161   551,398 females

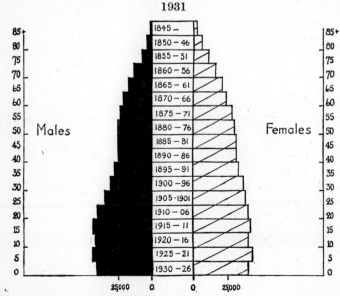

1931

pulation: 464,932 males   Total: 979,195   514,263 females

POPULATION OF SCOTLAND

(Reproduced from *Scottish Historical Review*, vol. xxviii.)

1871

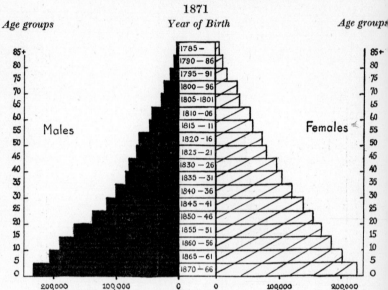

Population : 1,603,143 males   Total : 3,360,018   1,756,875 females

1931

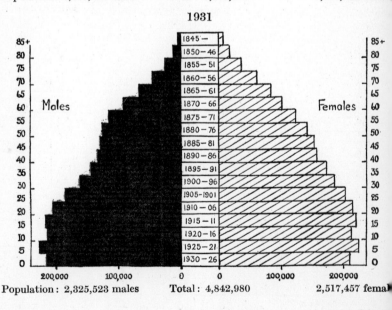

Population : 2,325,523 males   Total : 4,842,980   2,517,457 females

POPULATION OF GAIRLOCH

1861

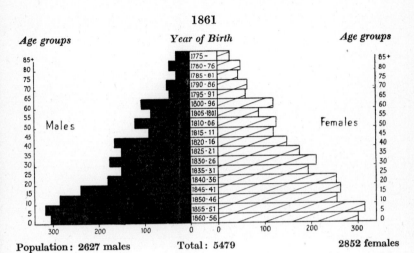

Age groups   *Year of Birth*   *Age groups*

Males   Females

Population: 2627 males   Total: 5479   2852 females

1931

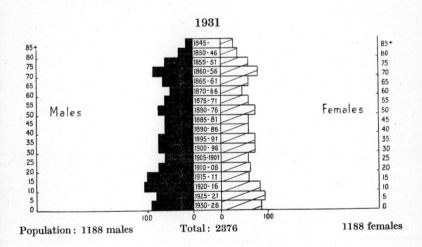

Males   Females

Population: 1188 males   Total: 2376   1188 females

WEBSTER'S CENSUS

EDITORIAL NOTE

The figures in this copy of Webster's Census are reproduced precisely as they appear in the original manuscript.

AN ACCOUNT

of the

NUMBER of PEOPLE in SCOTLAND

In the Year

One thousand Seven hundred and Fifty Five

by

ALEXANDER WEBSTER

One of the ministers of Edinburgh.

INDEX

INTRODUCTION

THE following Account of the Number of People in Scotland is the result of long and deliberate enquiry, and the Several Facts upon which it is founded are supported by the best Authority.

As few Parishes in Scotland keep distinct Registers of Births and Burials ; the Author was obliged to have recourse to a more laborious tho' more certain method of finding out the Number of Inhabitants.

He prevailed with the Society erected by Royal Charter for propagating Christian Knowledge in the Highlands and Islands of Scotland, to require every Minister within the Bounds of those Presbyteries where they had erected Charity Schools, to make and transmit a List of his Parishioners, distinguishing them into Protestants and Papists.

This Order was given under the Sanction of withdrawing the Schools in case of non-compliance. By this means and by various other methods taken to prevent mistakes, He obtained certain information of the exact number of Souls, throughout a great part of the Kingdom, and particularly in the more Northern Counties including the whole Highlands and Islands.

In the Year 1743, the Author prepared a Scheme which was afterwards ratified by Parliament for a Provision for the Widows and Children of Ministers &c. At that time He established a general Correspondence both with Clergy and Laity ; and this He now improved for obtaining from Ministers and Elders of those Parishes where the Society had erected no Schools, Lists either of Individuals or of Persons above a certain Age ; when the Lists contained only those above a certain Age, He calculated the Amount of the whole Inhabitants by the proportion which they might be supposed to bear to the number of Souls, according to the most approved Tables, compared with the Fact in many parts of Scotland, where the Ministers at his desire, not only numbered their Parishioners, but distinguished their respective Ages. So that it is humbly apprehended, the Account he has given of the Number of People, will be found to come very near the Truth, and to be sufficiently exact for answering every valuable purpose.

In the following Lists the several Shires or Countys in Scotland are placed according to the Map of the Country, and the Facts respecting them are stated in five Columns. The first column contains the names of the Parishes in an Alphabetical Order. The Second, the Extent of each Parish according to the ordinary computation of Miles in Scotland ; Two of which are nearly equal to Three English Miles. The third, the Number of Parishes and Ministers. The Fourth, the Number of Papists, Protestants and Inhabitants, and Column Fifth the Number of fighting Men in each Shire. To which is added an Abstract, Shewing not only the Total Number of People &c. but the Extent of each Shire or County, in English or Measured Miles, according to very accurate Maps, supposing a straight Line drawn between the places mentioned in Columns Fourth and Fifth of the Abstract.

The great Extent of many Parishes is occasioned by their running out into small narrow points, or from their being divided either by Mountains, Rivers, Arms of the Sea, or parts of other Parishes ; Some Parishes are so blended together as almost to double the Extent of each of them, computing from the one End to the other according to the method observed in the List.

By Fighting Men is meant those between Eighteen and Fifty six years of Age both Inclusive, whom the Author thinks with Doctor Halley, more properly deserve that name than those between Sixteen and Sixty ; The one being generally too weak to bear the fatigues of War and the weight of Arms ; and the other too Crazy and Infirm, notwithstanding some particular Instances have appeared to the contrary.

It appears from the Table which is Subjoined to the List of Inhabitants that 488,652 Persons in Scotland are under Eighteen years of age And 125,899 Persons above Fifty six which together make 614,551 ; This being Subtracted from 1,265,380 the Number of the whole Inhabitants, the

Remainder vizt. 650,829, are the Persons between those Ages of Eighteen and Fifty six ; At least one half of them may be reckoned Males, so that according to this computation, Scotland can raise of Fighting Men more than one Fourth of the Number of Souls which it contains. But as this proportion includes the Blind and Lame, or otherways diseased, the Author has supposed the Fighting Men in every Parish and Shire to be only one fifth part of the number of the Inhabitants, and these He is of opinion may be reckoned effective Men.

It only remains to be observed, that since the above enquiries have been made, the Number of People in several Parishes have varied somewhat, but not so much as to make any alteration of consequence in the general Plan ; Towns within these few years have become Populous and in certain places Country Parishes have diminished. A few Instances of the encrease of Towns will be found in the following List in the Footnotes placed under Edinburgh Glasgow Aberdeen &c.

D

| Berwick Shire | Extent | | Number of | | Number of Inhabitants | | | |
Parishes	Length	Breadth	Parishes	Ministers	Papists	Protestants	Total	Number of Fighting Men
Abbay St. Bathans	3	2	1	1		80	80	16
Ayton	3	2	1	1		797	797	$159\frac{3}{5}$
Bunkle & Preston	$3\frac{1}{2}$	3	1	1		691	691	$138\frac{1}{5}$
Coldinghame	5	$4\frac{1}{2}$	1	1		2313	2313	$462\frac{3}{5}$
Channelkirk	4	3	1	1		531	531	$106\frac{1}{5}$
Chirnside	$2\frac{3}{4}$	$1\frac{3}{4}$	1	1		383	383	$76\frac{4}{5}$
Cockburnspath	4	4	1	1		919	919	$183\frac{4}{5}$
Coldstream	5	4	1	1		1493	1493	$298\frac{3}{5}$
Cranshaws	4	2	1	1		214	214	$42\frac{4}{5}$
Dunse	$4\frac{1}{2}$	3	1	1		2593	2593	$518\frac{3}{5}$
Earlston	3	2	1	1		1197	1197	$239\frac{2}{5}$
Eccles	4	3	1	1		1489	1489	$297\frac{4}{5}$
Edrom	$6\frac{1}{2}$	$3\frac{1}{2}$	1	1		898	898	$179\frac{3}{5}$
Eymouth	$1\frac{1}{2}$	1	1	1		792	792	$158\frac{2}{5}$
Fogo	3	$1\frac{1}{2}$	1	1		566	566	$113\frac{1}{5}$
Foulden	$1\frac{1}{2}$	$\frac{3}{4}$	1	1		465	465	93
Greenlaw	4	3	1	1		895	895	179
Gordon	2	$1\frac{1}{2}$	1	1		737	737	$147\frac{2}{5}$
Hutton	2	2	1	1		751	751	$150\frac{1}{5}$
Carried Over			19	19		17804	17804	$3560\frac{4}{5}$

BERWICK SHIRE	Extent		Number of		Number of Inhabitants			
PARISHES	Length	Breadth	Parishes	Ministers	Papists	Protestants	Total	Number of Fighting Men
Brot. Over			19	19		17804	17804	3560$\frac{4}{5}$
Ladykirk	2$\frac{1}{2}$	1	1	1		386	386	77$\frac{1}{5}$
Langton	4	1	1	1		290	290	58
Lauder	9	4	1	1		1795	1795	359
Legerwood	2	2	1	1		398	398	79$\frac{3}{5}$
Longformacus	6	4	1	1		399	399	79$\frac{4}{5}$
Merton	2	1$\frac{1}{2}$	1	1		502	502	100$\frac{2}{5}$
Mordington	2$\frac{1}{2}$	1	1	1		181	181	36$\frac{1}{5}$
Nenthorn	2	1	1	1		497	497	99$\frac{2}{5}$
Polwarth	1	1	1	1		251	251	50$\frac{1}{5}$
Simprin [1]	2	1	1	1		143	143	28$\frac{3}{5}$
Swinton	2	1$\frac{1}{2}$	1	1		351	351	70$\frac{1}{5}$
Whitsome & Hilton	2$\frac{1}{2}$	1	1	1		399	399	79$\frac{4}{5}$
Westruther	3$\frac{1}{4}$	2$\frac{1}{2}$	1	1		591	591	118$\frac{1}{5}$
Total			32	32		23987	23987	4797$\frac{2}{5}$

[1] SIMPRIN—This Parish is now Suppressed and annexed to Swinton.

| HADINGTON SHIRE | Extent | | Number of | | | Number of Inhabitants | | |
PARISHES	Length	Breadth	Parishes	Ministers	Papists	Protestants	Total	Number of Fighting Men
Atholstonford	2½	1¼	1	1		691	691	138⅕
Bolton	3	1	1	1		359	359	71⅘
Dirlton	3	2	1	1		1700	1700	340
Garvald & Barra	4	2	1	1		774	774	154⅘
Hadington	6	6	1	2		3975	3975	795
Humbie & Keith	3½	3	1	1		1570	1570	314
Inverwick	8	4	1	1		941	941	188⅕
Morham	2	1	1	1		245	245	49
North Berwick	2	2	1	1		1412	1412	282⅖
Oldhamstocks	6	5	1	1		1022	1022	204⅖
Ormiston omitted	5 3	1½	1	1		622	622	124⅖
						810	810	162
Pencaitland	4	2	1	1		1310	1310	262
						910	910	182
Prestonkirk	6	2	1	1		1328	1328	265⅗
						1318	1318	263⅗
Prestonpans	2	2	1	1	2	1594	1596	319⅕
Saltoun	2	1	1	1		761	761	152⅕
Spott	6	2	1	1		727	727	145⅖
Stenton	7	3	1	1		631	631	126⅕
Tranent	3	2½	1	1		2459	2459	491⅘
Tyninghame [1]	3	2	1	1		599	599	119⅘
Whitekirk	2	1	1	1		369	369	73⅘
Carried Over			19	20	2	22467	22469	4493⅘

[1] TYNINGHAME—This Parish is now annexed to Whitekirk.

HADINGTON SHIRE	Extent		Number of		Number of Inhabitants			
PARISHES	Length	Breadth	Parishes	Ministers	Papists	Protestants	Total	Number of Fighting Men
Brot. Over			19	20	2	22467	22469	4493⅘
Whittinghame	8	3	1	1		1091	1091	218⅕
						714	714	142⅘
Yester	3	2	1	1		714	714	142⅘
						1091	1091	218⅕
Aberlady	2	1½	1	1		739	739	147⅘
Dunbar	5	1	1	1		3281	3281	656⅕
Gladsmuir	1½	1½	1	1		1415	1415	283
Total			24	25	2	29707	29709	5941⅘
EDINBURGH SHIRE								
Borthwick	4½	2½	1	1		910	910	182
Canongate	½	¼	1	2	20	4480	4500	900
Colington	2	1½	1	1		792	792	158⅖
Carington, vide Primrose			1	1		555	555	111
Corstorphine	2	2	1	1		995	995	199
Cockpen	2	1	1	1		640	640	128
Cramond	5	1½	1	1		1455	1455	291
						5	5	
Cranston	3	2	1	1	4	721	725	145
Creighton	3	2½	1	1		611	611	122⅕
Currie	4	3	1	1		1227	1227	245⅖
Carried Over			9	10	24	11831	11855	2371

[1] EDINBURGH—The Papists who reside in Edinburgh and its Liberties being generally Persons in low life such as Chairmen &c. their precise number cannot be ascertained but they will at least amount to the number stated. It is alledged that the Number of Inhabitants has encreased within the City since the Extention of its Royalty :

EDINBURGH SHIRE	Extent		Number of		Number of Inhabitants			
PARISHES	Length	Breadth	Parishes	Ministers	Papists	Protestants	Total	Number of Fighting Men
Brot. Over			9	10	24	11831	11855	2371
Dalkeith	1	$\frac{1}{2}$	1	1		3110	3110	622
Duddingston	3	1	1	1		989	989	$197\frac{4}{5}$
Edinburgh [1]	1	1	10	16	200	30922	31122	$6224\frac{2}{5}$
(for note see p. 14)	$\frac{1}{2}$	$\frac{1}{4}$	9					
Fala & Soutra	3	1	1	1		312	312	$62\frac{2}{5}$
Glencross	3	3	1	1		557	557	$111\frac{2}{5}$
Herriot	4	2	1	1		209	209	$41\frac{4}{5}$
Inveresk	$1\frac{3}{4}$	$1\frac{1}{2}$	1	1		4645	4645	929
Kirknewton	3	2	1	1		1157	1157	$231\frac{2}{5}$
Laswade	4	2	1	1		2190	2190	438
Libberton	4	3	1	1		2793	2793	$558\frac{3}{5}$
	3	3					3457	
							2793	
Leith North	1	$\frac{1}{4}$	1	1	4	2201	2205	441
Leith South	1	$\frac{1}{2}$	1	2	10	7190	7200	1440
Mid Calder	5	4	1	1		1369	1369	$273\frac{4}{5}$
Newton	$2\frac{1}{2}$	$1\frac{1}{2}$	1	1		1199	1199	$239\frac{4}{5}$
Newbottle	3	2	1	1		1439	1439	$287\frac{4}{5}$
Pennycook	4	3	1	1		890	890	178
Primrose or Carrington	3	2	1	1		555	555	111
Ratho	4	2	1	1		930	930	186
Carried Over			36	44	238	74488	74726	$14945\frac{1}{5}$

but this is by no means the case. It is certain that the New Town does not contain many more houses than what have been taken down in the Old Town for widening its Streets &c. If to this is added the great number of Families who now reside in St. Cuthberts parish from Edinr. it is thought the above number will be rather above than below the fact. Vide next page.

EDINBURGH SHIRE	Extent		Number of		Number of Inhabitants			
PARISHES	Length	Breadth	Parishes	Ministers	Papists	Protestants	Total	Number of Fighting Men
Brot. Over			36	44	238	74488	74726	14945$\frac{1}{5}$
St. Cuthberts [1]	3$\frac{1}{2}$	3	1	2	25	12168	12193	2438$\frac{3}{5}$
Stow	10	5	1	1		1294	1294	258$\frac{4}{5}$
Temple	5	2	1	1		905	905	181
West Calder	7	5	1	1		1294	1294	258$\frac{4}{5}$
Total			40	49	263	90149	90412	18082$\frac{2}{5}$
LINLITHGOW SHIRE								
Abercorn	3	1$\frac{1}{2}$	1	1		1037	1037	207$\frac{2}{5}$
Borrowstonness	2	1$\frac{3}{4}$	1	1		2668	2668	533$\frac{3}{5}$
Bathgate	5	2$\frac{1}{2}$	1	1		1594	1594	318$\frac{4}{5}$
Carridden	3	1$\frac{1}{2}$	1	1		1164	1164	232$\frac{4}{5}$
Dalmeny	5	2	1	1		1103	1103	220$\frac{3}{5}$
Ecclesmahan	2$\frac{1}{2}$	$\frac{1}{2}$	1	1		351	351	70$\frac{1}{5}$
Kirkliston	4	2$\frac{3}{4}$	1	1		1461	1461	292$\frac{1}{5}$
Linlithgow	4	3$\frac{1}{2}$	1	1		3296	3296	659$\frac{1}{5}$
Livingston	3	1$\frac{1}{2}$	1	1		598	598	119$\frac{3}{5}$
Carried Over			9	10		13272	13272	2551$\frac{2}{5}$

[1] ST. CUTHBERTS—This Parish almost surrounds the City of Edinburgh. It lyes upon the South, West and North of it, and is more encreased in Population by the late improvements than any other part of the City or its Environs. By a late Account taken with a good deal of care St. Cuthberts contains about 7200 Houses, which computing at five to a House makes the Inhabitants amount to 36000.

LINLITHGOW SHIRE	Extent		Number of		Number of Inhabitants			
PARISHES	Length	Breadth	Parishes	Ministers	Papists	Protestants	Total	Number of Fighting Men
Brot. Over			9	10		13272	13272	2654⅖
Torphichen	7	2	1	1		1295	1295	259
Queensferry	½	¹⁄₁₆	1	1		451	451	90⅕
Uphall	2	1½	1	1		690	690	138
Whitburn	4	2	1	1		1121	1121	224⅕
Total			13	14		16829	16829	3365⅘
PEEBLES SHIRE								
Broughton	2½	2½	1	1		367	367	73⅖
Drumelzier	6	½	1	1		305	305	61
Eddleston	7	6	1	1		679	679	135⅘
Glenholm	5½	1½	1	1		392	392	78⅖
Inverleithen	7	4	1	1		559	559	111⅘
Kilbucho	3½	2½	1	1		279	279	55⅘
Kirkurd	4	2	1	1		310	310	62
Linton	5	3	1	1		831	831	166⅕
Lyne	3	2	1	1		265	265	53
Carried Over			9	9		3987	3987	797⅖

PEEBLES SHIRE	Extent		Number of		Number of Inhabitants			
PARISHES	Length	Breadth	Parishes	Ministers	Papists	Protestants	Total	Number of Fighting Men
Brot. Over			9	9		3987	3987	797$\frac{2}{5}$
Manner	6	4	1	1		320	320	64
Newlands	8	4	1	1		1009	1009	201$\frac{4}{5}$
Peebles	2	2	1	1		1896	1896	379$\frac{1}{5}$
Skirling	2$\frac{1}{2}$	1$\frac{1}{2}$	1	1		335	335	67
Stobo	3	2$\frac{1}{2}$	1	1	1	312	313	62$\frac{3}{5}$
Traquair	5	3	1	1	21	630	651	130$\frac{1}{5}$
Tweedsmuir	8	6	1	1		397	397	79$\frac{2}{5}$
Total			16	16	22	8886	8908	1781$\frac{3}{5}$
SELKIRK SHIRE								
Etterick	8	4	1	1		397	397	79$\frac{2}{5}$
Roberton [1]	8	4	1	1		651	651	130$\frac{1}{5}$
Selkirk	8	7	1	1		1793	1793	358$\frac{3}{5}$
Yarrow	12	12	1	1		1180	1180	236
Total			4	4		4021	4021	804$\frac{1}{5}$

[1] ROBERTOUN—Part of this Parish lyes in Roxburgh Shire.

Roxburgh Shire	Extent		Number of			Number of Inhabitants		
Parishes	Length	Breadth	Parishes	Ministers	Papists	Protestants	Total	Number of Fighting Men
Abbotrule [1]	2	1½	1	1		189	189	37⅘
Ancrum	4	4	1	1		1066	1066	213⅕
Ashkirk [2]	4	1	1	1		629	629	125⅘
Bedrule	2½	1	1	1		297	297	59⅖
Bowden	4	2	1	1		672	672	134⅖
Canonby	9	3½	1	1		1733	1733	346⅗
Castleton	12	4	1	1		1507	1507	301⅖
Cavers	15	4	1	1		993	993	198⅗
Creline	1	¾	1	1		387	387	77⅖
Eckford	3	3	1	1		1083	1083	216⅗
Ednem	2	2	1	1		387	387	77⅖
Ewis	6	2½	1	1		392	392	78⅖
Galashiels	3½	2½	1	1		998	998	199⅗
Hawick	11	1½	1	1		2713	2713	542⅗
Hobkirk			1	1		530	530	106
Hownam	3	2	1	1		632	632	126⅖
Jedburgh	9	6	1	1		5816	5816	1163⅕
Kelso	2	1½	1	1		2781	2781	556⅕
Kirkton	6	½	1	1		330	330	66
Carried Over			19	19		23135	23135	4627

[1] ABBOTRULE—This Parish is now suppressed & annexed to the Parishes of Hobkirk and Southdean.

[2] ASHKIRK—Part of this Parish lyes in Selkirk Shire.

Roxburgh Shire	Extent		Number of		Number of Inhabitants			
Parishes	Length	Breadth	Parishes	Ministers	Papists	Protestants	Total	Number of Fighting Men
Brot. Over			19	19		23135	23135	4627
Lessudden	2	1	1	1		309	309	$61\frac{4}{5}$
Lilliesleaf	3	3	1	1		521	521	$104\frac{4}{5}$
Linton	$3\frac{1}{2}$	$1\frac{1}{2}$	1	1		413	413	$82\frac{3}{5}$
Mackerston	2	1	1	1		165	165	33
Maxton	3	$1\frac{1}{2}$	1	1		397	397	$79\frac{2}{5}$
Melrose	9	4	1	1		2322	2322	$464\frac{2}{5}$
Minto	$2\frac{1}{2}$	2	1	1		395	395	79
Morbattle	7	3	1	1		789	789	$157\frac{4}{5}$
Oxnam	5	$2\frac{1}{2}$	1	1		760	760	152
Roxburgh	4	2	1	1		784	784	$156\frac{4}{5}$
Smalholm	3	2	1	1		551	551	$110\frac{1}{5}$
Southdean			1	1		480	480	96
Sprouston	4	2	1	1		1089	1089	$217\frac{4}{5}$
Stitchill	2	2	1	1		959	959	$191\frac{4}{5}$
Wilton	2	2	1	1		936	936	$187\frac{1}{4}$
Yetholm	$2\frac{1}{2}$	1	1	1		699	699	$139\frac{4}{5}$
Total			35	35		34704	34704	$6940\frac{4}{5}$

Dumfries Shire	Extent		Number of		Number of Inhabitants			
Parishes	Length	Breadth	Parishes	Ministers	Papists	Protestants	Total	Number of Fighting Men
Annan	5	4	1	1		1498	1498	299 3/5
Applegirth	5	4	1	1	2	895	897	179 2/5
Carlaverock	4	2	1	1	4	780	784	156 4/5
Closeburn	8	7	1	1		999	999	199 4/5
Cummertrees	5½	3½	1	1	1	630	631	126 1/5
Dalton	4	2½	1	1		451	451	90 1/5
Dornock	3½	2	1	1		716	716	143 1/5
Drysdale	5	4	1	1		1097	1097	219 2/5
Dumfries	6	2	1	2	22	4495	4517	903 2/5
Dunscore	9	3½	1	1		651	651	130 1/5
Durrisdeer	8	4	1	1		1097 1019	1097 1019	219 2/5 203 4/5
Eskdalemuir	9	7	1	1		597 675	597 675	119 2/5 135
Glencairn	13	3	1	1		1794	1794	358 4/5
Graitny	4	2½	1	1		1051	1051	210 1/5
Hoddam	4	4	1	1	1	1392	1393	278 3/5
Holywood	6	1	1	1		596	596	119 1/5
Hutton	9	6	1	1		993	993	198 3/5
Johnston	6	4	1	1		494	494	98 4/5
Keir	6	1	1	1		495	495	99
Carried Over			19	20	30	20721	20751	4150 1/5

Dumfries Shire	Extent		Number of		Number of Inhabitants			
PARISHES	Length	Breadth	Parishes	Ministers	Papists	Protestants	Total	Number of Fighting Men
Brot. Over			19	20	30	20721	20751	4150$\frac{1}{4}$
Kirkconnel	10	6	1	1		899	899	179$\frac{4}{5}$
Kirkmahoe	10	6	1	1		1098	1098	219$\frac{3}{5}$
Kirkmichael	9	4	1	1		894	894	178$\frac{4}{5}$
Kirkpatrick-Juxta	6$\frac{1}{2}$	5$\frac{1}{2}$	1	1		794	794	158$\frac{4}{5}$
Kirkpatrick-Fleming	6	4	1	1	1	1146	1147	229$\frac{2}{5}$
Langholm	5	5	1	1		1833	1833	366$\frac{3}{5}$
Lochmaben	3	2	1	1		1395	1395	279
Middlebie	8	4	1	1		991	991	198$\frac{1}{5}$
Moffat	13	6	1	1	1	1611	1612	322$\frac{2}{5}$
Morton	3	2	1	1		435	435	87
Mouswald	4$\frac{1}{2}$	4	1	1	3	550	553	110$\frac{3}{5}$
Penpont	12	3	1	1		838	838	167$\frac{3}{5}$
Ruthwell	5	4	1	1		599	599	119$\frac{4}{5}$
Sanquhar	13	6	1	1		1998	1998	399$\frac{3}{5}$
St. Mungo	3	1$\frac{1}{2}$	1	1		481	481	96$\frac{1}{5}$
Tinwald	3$\frac{1}{2}$	3$\frac{1}{2}$	1	1		795	795	159
Torthorwald	6	2	1	1		584	584	116$\frac{4}{5}$
Tynron	7	2	1	1		464	464	92$\frac{4}{5}$
Carried Over			37	38	35	38126	38161	7632$\frac{1}{5}$

Dumfries Shire	Extent		Number of		Number of Inhabitants			
PARISHES	Length	Breadth	Parishes	Ministers	Papists	Protestants	Total	Number of Fighting Men
Brot. Over			37	38	35	38126	38161	7632⅕
Tundergirth	8	1	1	1		625	625	125
Wamphray	4	2	1	1		458	458	91⅗
Westerkirk	7	6	1	1		544	544	108⅘
Total			40	41	35	39753	39788	7957⅗
SHIRE OF KIRKCUDBRIGHT								
Anwoth	6	2	1	1		531	531	106⅕
Balmaclellan	6	4	1	1		534	534	106⅘
Balmaghie	10	5	1	1		697	697	139⅖
Borgue	5	4	1	1		697	697	139⅖
Buittle	7	4	1	1	85	814	899	179⅘
Carsphairn	10	10	1	1		609	609	121⅘
Colvend	4	3	1	1	12	886	898	179⅗
Crossmichael	4	2	1	1		613	613	122⅗
Dalry	14	6	1	1		891	891	178⅕
Girthon	14½	4	1	1		367	367	73⅖
Carried Over			10	10	97	6639	6736	1347⅕

KIRKCUDBRIGHT SHIRE	Extent		Number of		Number of Inhabitants			
PARISHES	Length	Breadth	Parishes	Ministers	Papists	Protestants	Total	Number of Fighting Men
Brot. Over			10	10	97	6639	6736	1347 1/5
Irongray	6	4	1	1		895	895	179
Kells	12	4	1	1	4	780	784	156 4/5
Kelton	6	4	1	1	2	809	811	162 1/5
Kirkbean	4	2	1	1	7	522	529	105 4/5
Kirkgunzeon	5	4	1	1		489	489	97 4/5
Kirkcudbright	6	3	1	1	10	1503	1513	302 3/5
Kirkmabrick	7	4	1	1		858	858	171 3/5
Kirkpatrick Durham	9	3	1	1		699	699	139 4/5
Lochrutton	4	2	1	1		564	564	112 4/5
Minnigaff	17 1/2	8 1/2	1	1		1209	1209	241 4/5
New Abbay	7	2	1	1	4	630	634	126 4/5
Parton	4	4	1	1	16	380	396	79 1/5
Rerrick	8	6	1	1	3	1048	1051	210 1/5
Terreagles	3	2 1/2	1	1	42	355	397	79 2/5
Tongland	6	3	1	1	1	536	537	107 2/5
Troqueer	6	2 1/2	1	1	118	1273	1391	278 1/5
Twynholm	6	2	1	1		519	519	103 4/5
Urr	10	6	1	1	45	1148	1193	238 3/5
Total			28	28	349	20856	21205	4241

WIGTOWN SHIRE	Extent		Number of		Number of Inhabitants			
PARISHES	Length	Breadth	Parishes	Ministers	Papists	Protestants	Total	Number of Fighting Men
Glasserton	4	3	1	1		809	809	161⅘
Glenluce	8	6	1	1		1509	1509	301⅘
Inch	7	5	1	1		1513	1513	302⅗
Kirkcolm	4½	3½	1	1		765	765	153
Kirkcowan	13	4	1	1		795	795	159
Kirkinner	5	4	1	1		792	792	158⅖
Kirkmaiden	8	3	1	1		1051	1051	210⅕
Leswalt	5	3	1	1		652	652	130⅖
Mochrum	10	4	1	1		828	828	165⅗
Newluce	8	4	1	1		459	459	91⅘
Penninghame	12	4	1	1		1509	1509	301⅘
Portpatrick	3	2	1	1		611	611	122⅕
Sorbie	4	3	1	1		968	968	193⅗
Stonykirk	8	5¼	1	1		1151	1151	230⅕
Stranrawer	⅓	⅕	1	1		610	610	122
Wigtown	4	4	1	1		1032	1032	206⅖
Whithorn	5	3	1	1		1412	1412	282⅖
Total			17	17		16466	16466	3293⅕

Air Shire	Extent		Number of		Number of Inhabitants			
Parishes	Length	Breadth	Parishes	Ministers	Papists	Protestants	Total	Number of Fighting Men
Air	3	2	1	2		2964	2964	592⅘
Auchinleck	10	2	1	1		887	887	177⅖
Ardrossan	4	2	1	1		1297	1297	259⅖
Ballintrae	6	5	1	1		1049	1049	209⅘
Barr	9	7	1	1		858	858	171⅗
Beith	4	3	1	1		2064	2064	412⅘
Calmonell	14	4	1	1		1814	1814	362⅘
Coylton	7	3	1	1		527	527	105⅖
Craigie	4	1	1	1		551	551	110⅕
Daily	6	2	1	1		839	839	167⅘
Dalmellington	8	3	1	1		739	739	147⅘
Dalry	7	6	1	1		1498	1498	299⅗
Dalrymple	5	2	1	1		439	439	87⅘
Dreghorn	6	1½	1	1		887	887	177⅖
Dundonald	4½	4½	1	1		983	983	196⅗
Dunlop	5	2	1	1		796	796	159⅕
Fenwick	6	3	1	1		1113	1113	222⅗
Galston	7	2	1	1		1013	1013	202⅗
Girvan	6	4	1	1		1193	1193	238⅗
Carried Over			19	20		21511	21511	4302⅕

| AIR SHIRE | Extent | | Number of | | Number of Inhabitants | | | |
PARISHES	Length	Breadth	Parishes	Ministers	Papists	Protestants	Total	Number of Fighting Men
Brot. Over			19	20		21511	21511	4302$\frac{1}{5}$
Irvine	3	2	1	1		4025	4025	805
Kilbirnie	3	2	1	1		651	651	130$\frac{1}{5}$
Kilbride	5	2	1	1		885	885	177
Kilmaurs	4	2	1	1		1094	1094	880$\frac{3}{5}$
Kilmarnock	7	3	1	2		4403	4403	508$\frac{1}{5}$
Kilwinning	5$\frac{1}{2}$	3	1	1		2541	2541	218$\frac{4}{5}$
Kirkmichael	6 6	5 2	1	1		710	710	142
Kirkoswald	6 6	2 5	1	1		1168	1168	233$\frac{3}{5}$
Loudoun	6	2	1	1		1494	1494	298$\frac{4}{5}$
Largs	9	4	1	1		1164	1164	232$\frac{4}{5}$
Maybole	7	4	1	1		2058	2058	411$\frac{3}{5}$
Mauchline	5	2	1	1		1169	1169	233$\frac{4}{5}$
Monkton	3	2	1	1		1163	1163	232$\frac{3}{5}$
Muirkirk	7	7	1	1		745	745	149
New Cumnock	10$\frac{1}{2}$	7$\frac{1}{2}$	1	1		1467 1497	1467 1497	293$\frac{2}{5}$ 299$\frac{2}{5}$
Newton upon Air [1]			1	1				
Ochiltree	4	4	1	1		1210	1210	242
Old Cumnock	5	2	1	1		1366 1336	1366 1336	273$\frac{1}{5}$ 267$\frac{1}{5}$
Carried Over			37	39		48824	48824	9764$\frac{4}{5}$

[1] NEWTON upon AIR—This is a New Erection ; The Inhabitants are included in those stated as living in the Town of Air.

AIR SHIRE	Extent		Number of			Number of Inhabitants		
PARISHES	Length	Breadth	Parishes	Ministers	Papists	Protestants	Total	Number of Fighting Men
Brot. Over			37	39		48824	48824	9764$\frac{4}{5}$
Riccarton	4$\frac{1}{2}$	2	1	1		745	745	149
St. Quivox	3	2	1	1		499	499	99$\frac{4}{5}$
Sorn	6	4	1	1		1494	1494	298$\frac{4}{5}$
Stair	4	3	1	1		369	369	73$\frac{4}{5}$
Stevenston	2	1	1	1		1412	1412	282$\frac{2}{5}$
Stewarton	7	3	1	1		2819	2819	563$\frac{4}{5}$
Straiton	16	6	1	1		1123	1123	224$\frac{3}{5}$
Symington	3	1	1	1		359	359	71$\frac{4}{5}$
Tarbolton	5$\frac{1}{2}$	2$\frac{1}{2}$	1	1		1365	1365	273
Total			46	48		59009	59009	11801$\frac{4}{5}$
LANERK SHIRE								
Biggar	4	3	1	1		1098	1098	219$\frac{3}{5}$
Blantyre	5	1	1	1		496	496	99$\frac{1}{5}$
Bothwell	6	3	1	1		1561	1561	312$\frac{1}{5}$
Calder	12	2	1	1		2396	2396	479$\frac{1}{5}$
Carried Over			4	4		5551	5551	1110$\frac{1}{5}$

LANERK SHIRE	Extent		Number of		Number of Inhabitants			
PARISHES	Length	Breadth	Parishes	Ministers	Papists	Protestants	Total	Number of Fighting Men
Brot. Over			4	4		5551	5551	1110⅕
Cambuslang	3	3	1	1		934	934	186⅘
Cambusnethan	9	3	1	1		1419	1419	283⅘
Carluke	5	4	1	1		1459	1459	291⅘
Carmichael	4	2	1	1		899	899	179⅘
Carmannock	4	1½	1	1		471	471	98⅕
Carnwath	7	6	1	1		2845 2390	2845 2390	569 478
Carstairs	4	2	1	1		422 843	422 843	84⅖ 169
Coulter	3	2	1	1		390 422	390 422	78 84⅖
Covington	2	1¼	1	1		521	521	104⅕
Crawfurd-John	8	2½	1	1		765	765	153
Crawfurdmuir	12	10	1	1		2009	2009	401⅘
Dalserf	3½	2	1	1		765	765	153
Dalziel	3	1	1	1		351	351	70⅕
Dolphington	2	2	1	1		302	302	60⅖
Dowglas	9	3	1	1		2009	2009	401⅘
Dunsyre	4	3	1	1		359	359	71⅘
Glasgow [1]	1¼	1	8 6	8 6		23546	23546	4709⅕
Do. Barony Parish	6	3½	1	1		3905	3905	781
Carried Over			29	29		48922	48922	9784⅖

[1] GLASGOW—It appears by the Bills of Mortality that the Inhabitants have encreased to nearly double the Number stated above.

Lanerk Shire	Extent		Number of		Number of Inhabitants			
Parishes	Length	Breadth	Parishes	Ministers	Papists	Protestants	Total	Number of Fighting Men
Brot. Over			29	29		48922	48922	9784$\frac{2}{5}$
Glasgow Gorbals Parish [1]			1	1				
Glasford	5	2	1	1		559	559	111$\frac{4}{5}$
Govan	5	2$\frac{1}{2}$	1	1		4389	4389	877$\frac{4}{5}$
Hamilton	5	5	1	2	2	3813	3815	763
Kilbride	10	4	1	1		2029	2029	405$\frac{4}{5}$
Lamington	5	4	1	1		599	599	119$\frac{4}{5}$
Lanerk	3	3	1	1		2294	2294	458$\frac{4}{5}$
	4	2						
Lesmahagow	8	8	1	2		3996	3996	799$\frac{1}{5}$
	See Stat Acct. V 7. 430 Qy					2996		
Libberton	4	2	1	1		738	738	147$\frac{3}{5}$
	3	3						
Monkland East	7	4	1	1		2713	2713	542$\frac{3}{5}$
Do. West	7	3	1	1		1813	1813	362$\frac{3}{5}$
Pettenain	2	2	1	1		330	330	66
Robertoun [2]	4	1	1	1		511	511	102$\frac{1}{5}$
Rutherglen	1$\frac{1}{2}$	1$\frac{1}{4}$	1	1		988	988	197$\frac{3}{5}$
Shotts	8	5	1	1		2322	2322	464$\frac{2}{5}$
Stonehouse	4$\frac{1}{2}$	3	1	1		823	823	164$\frac{3}{5}$
Strathaven	11	8	1	1		3551	3551	710$\frac{1}{5}$
Symington	2	1	1	1		264	264	52$\frac{4}{5}$
Carried Over			47	49	2	80754	80756	16131$\frac{1}{5}$

[1] Gorbals—This is a new Eerection ; The Inhabitants are included in those states as being in the Parish of Govan.

[2] Robertoun—This Parish is now Suppressed & Annexed to Wiston.

Lanerk Shire	Extent		Number of		Number of Inhabitants			
Parishes	Length	Breadth	Parishes	Ministers	Papists	Protestants	Total	Number of Fighting Men
Brot. Over			47	49	2	80754	80756	16131⅕
Walston	2	2	1	1		479	479	95⅘
Wiston	4	2½	1	1		591	591 511 1102	118⅕
Total			49	51	2	81724	81726	16345⅕
Renfrew Shire								
Eaglesham	4¾	3¼	1	1		1103	1103	220⅗
Eastwood	4	3	1	1		1142	1142	228⅖
Erskine	5	2	1	1	2	827	829	165⅘
Greenock Old Parish	3½	3	1	1		1886	1886	377⅕
Do. New Parish	3	2	1	1		1972	1972	394⅖
Houstoun	3	1½	1	1		451	451	90⅕
Inchinan	2	1	1	1		397	397	79⅖
Innerkip	5	2	1	1		1590	1590	318
Killallan [1]	4	1½	1	1		496	496	99⅕
Kilbarchan	6	2	1	1		1485	1485	297
Kilmalcolm	5	3	1	1		1495	1495	299
Carried Over			11	11	2	12844	12846	2569⅕

[1] KILLALLAN—Is now Suppressed and Annexed to Houstoun.

RENFREW SHIRE	Extent		Number of		Number of Inhabitants			
PARISHES	Length	Breadth	Parishes	Ministers	Papists	Protestants	Total	Number of Fighting Men
Brot. Over			11	11	2	12844	12846	2569¼
Cathcart ¹	2½	1½	1	1		499	499	99⅘
Lochwinnoch	6	5	1	1		1530	1530	306
Mcarns	5½	2	1	1		886	886	177¼
Neilston	7	4	1	1		1299	1299	259⅘
Paisley Abbay Parish ⎫₂	8	3	1	2	1	2508	2509	501⅘
Paisley Town parish ⎭	1	1 ½	1	3 2		4290	4290	858
Port Glasgow	2	2	1	1		1695	1695	339
Renfrew	2	2	1	1		1091	1091	218⅘
Total			19	22	3	26642	26645	5329
BUTE SHIRE								
Cumbry Island	3	1½	1	1		259	259	51⅘
Kilbride in Arran	18	3	1	1		1369	1369	273⅘
Kilmorie in Arran	24	4	1	1		2277	2277	455⅖
Kingarth	5	3	1	1		998	998	199⅗
Rothsay	7	3	1	1		2222	2222	444⅖
Total			5	5		7125	7125	1425

¹ CATHCART—Parts of this Parish lyes in Lanerk Shire.

² PAISLEY—From the rapid progress of Manufactures in this Town, the Inhabitants now amount to above 20000.

ARGYLE	Extent		Number of		Number of Inhabitants			
PARISHES	Length	Breadth	Parishes	Ministers	Papists	Protestants	Total	Number of Fighting Men
Ardchatton	15	$4\frac{1}{2}$	1	1	3	2192	2195	439
Ardnamurchan [1]			1	1	2300	2700	5000	1000
Campbelton [2]	13	10	1	2	15	4582	4597	$919\frac{2}{5}$
Coll	12	4	1	1		1193	1193	$238\frac{3}{5}$
Colonsay	7	$1\frac{1}{2}$	1	1		1097	1097	$219\frac{2}{5}$
Craignish	6	2	1	1		769	769	$153\frac{4}{5}$
Dunoon	16	5	1	1		1757	1757	$351\frac{3}{5}$
Gigha	6	2	1	1		514	514	$102\frac{4}{5}$
Glenorchy	25	8	1	1	4	1650	1654	$330\frac{4}{5}$
Inverchaolan	8	7	1	1		944	944	$188\frac{4}{5}$
Glenary	8	3	1	1		2751	2751	$550\frac{1}{5}$
Inverary	4	2	1	1				
Kilbrandon			1	1		1492	1492	$298\frac{2}{5}$
Kilcalmonell [3]	14	$4\frac{1}{2}$	1	1		1925	1925	385
Kilchrenan	11	6	1	1		1030	1030	206
Kilchoman (In Islay)								
Kildalton (In Islay)			1	1		5344	5344	$1068\frac{4}{5}$
Killarow (In Islay)			1	1				
Kilfinan	11	3	1	1		1793	1793	$358\frac{3}{5}$
Carried Over			19	19	2322	31733	34055	6811

[1] ARDNAMURCHAN—This Parish consists of FiveCountrys, Moidart 24 Miles long 7 Broad ; Ardnamurchan and Swinart which together are 32 long & 6 Broad ; Arisaig 24 Long & 7 or 8 Broad & Morar 18 Long & 8 Broad. Moidart Arisaig & Morar lye in Inverness Shire. The number of Inhabitants cannot absolutely be depended on nor is it known whether those employed about the Mines of Strontian generally about 5, or 600, are included in the 5000.

[2] CAMPBELTON—A considerable number of Papists come to this Parish during the Fishing Season.

[3] KILCALMONELL—Kilberry tho' divided by an arm of the Sea Nine computed Miles long is annexed to it.

ARGYLE SHIRE	Extent		Number of		Number of Inhabitants			
PARISHES	Length	Breadth	Parishes	Ministers	Papists	Protestants	Total	Number of Fighting Men
Brot. Over			19	19	2322	31733	34055	6811
Kilfinchen	15	8	1	1		1685	1685	337
Killean	16	8	1	1		2391	2391	478⅕
Kilmanivaig	24	20	1	1	1400	1595	2995	599
Kilmartine	10	3	1	1		1150	1150	230
Kilmodan	6	½	1	1	1	805	806	161⅕
Kilmichael	15	8	1	1	1	2750	2751	550⅕
Kilmore	10	7	1	1		1200	1200	240
Kilninian	12	12	1	1	5	2585	2590	518
Kilninver	7½	7	1	1		1045	1045	209
Lismore & Appin	34	12	1	1		2812	2812	562⅖
Lochgoilhead	15	9½	1	1	1	1504	1505	301
Morven	18	9	1	1	6	1217	1223	244⅗
North Knapdale	10	7	1	1		1369	1369	273⅘
Skipness	21	5½	1	1		1369	1369	273⅘
Southend	10	5	1	1	6	1385	1391	278⅕
South Knapdale	19	10	1	1		1292	1292	258⅖
Small Isles [1]			1	1	582	361	943	188⅗
Strachur	17	4	1	1		1193	1193	238⅗
Carried Over			37	37	4324	59441	63765	12753

[1] SMALL ISLES—This Parish consists of the Island of Egg which is 4 miles long & 2 broad, contains 29 Protestants 316 Papists & lyes in the Shire of Inverness; Rum 8 miles long 6 Broad 194 Protestants 12 Papists; Muck 2 miles long 1 Broad 130 Protestants 31 Papists & Cana 3 Miles long 1 Broad 8 Pro-

ARGYLE SHIRE	Extent		Number of		Number of Inhabitants			
PARISHES	Length	Breadth	Parishes	Ministers	Papists	Protestants	Total	Number of Fighting Men
Brot. Over			37	37	4324	59441	63765	12753
Torosay	14	9	1	1	2	1010	1012	202⅔
Tiree	8	1¼	1	1	3	1506	1509 1193 2702	301⅘
Total			39	39	4329	61957	66286	13257½
SHIRE OF DUMBARTON								
Arroquhar	15	4	1	1		466	466	93⅕
Bonhill	6	4	1	1		901	901	180⅕
Cardross	5	1	1	1		795	795	159
Cumbernauld	8	7	1	1		2303	2303	460⅗
Dumbarton	5	2	1	1		1480	1480	296
Kilpatrick East	5	4	1	1		1390	1390	278
Do. West	5	2½	1	1		1281	1281	256⅕
Kilmaronock			1	1		1193	1193	238⅗
Kirkintilloch	4	2	1	1		1696	1696	339⅕
Luss	9	6	1	1		978	978	195⅗
Carried Over			10	10		12483	12483	2496⅗

testants & 223 Papists.   These three last Islands lye in the Shire of Argyle.

Dumbarton Shire	Extent		Number of		Number of Inhabitants			
Parishes	Length	Breadth	Parishes	Ministers	Papists	Protestants	Total	Number of Fighting Men
Brot. Over			10	10		12483	12483	$2496\frac{3}{5}$
Roseneath	5	2	1	1		521	521	$104\frac{1}{5}$
Row	10	3	1	1		853	853	$170\frac{3}{5}$
Total			12	12		13857	13857	$2771\frac{2}{5}$
Stirling Shire								
Airth	$3\frac{1}{2}$	2	1	1		2316	2316	$463\frac{1}{5}$
Alva	$3\frac{1}{2}$	2	1	1		436	436	$87\frac{1}{5}$
Baldernock	3	8 3	1	1		621	621	$124\frac{1}{5}$
Balfron	7	$1\frac{1}{2}$	1	1		755	755	151
Bothkennar	2	1	1	1		529	529	$105\frac{4}{5}$
Buchanan	18	9	1	1	7	1692	1699	$339\frac{4}{5}$
Campsie	5	4	1	1		1399	1399	$279\frac{4}{5}$
Denny	4	2	1	1		1392	1392	$278\frac{2}{5}$
Drymen	9	$7\frac{1}{2}$	1	1		2789	2789	$557\frac{4}{5}$
Falkirk	6	4	1	1		3932	3932	$786\frac{2}{5}$
Fintry	4	4	1	1	1	890	891	$178\frac{1}{5}$
Carried Over			11	11	8	16751	16759	$3351\frac{4}{5}$

Stirling Shire	Extent		Number of		Number of Inhabitants			
Parishes	Length	Breadth	Parishes	Ministers	Papists	Protestants	Total	Number of Fighting Men
Brot. Over			11	11	8	16751	16759	3351 4/5
Gargunnock	4	4	1	1		956	956	191 1/5
Killearn	8	2	1	1		959	959	191 4/5
Kilsyth	5	3	1	1		1395	1395	279
Larbert	7	1½	1	1		1864	1864	372 4/5
Muiravonside	5	3	1	1		1539	1539	307 4/5
Polmont	3	2	1	1		1094	1094	218 4/5
Slamannan	6	3	1	1		1209	1209	241 4/5
Stirling	1½	½	1	2		3951	3951	790 1/5
St. Ninians	10	5½	1	1		6491	6491	1298 1/5
Strathblane	4	3	1	1		797	797	159 2/5
Total			21	22	8	37006	37014	7402 4/5

Clackmanan Shire								
Alloa	3	3	1	1	2	5814	4653 5816	1163 1/5
Clackmanan	3½	2½	1	1		1913	1913	382 3/5
Dollar	4	2	1	1		517	517	103 2/5
Tillicoultry	2	1	1	1		757	757	151 2/5
Total			4	4	2	9001	9003	1800 3/5

Kinross Shire	Extent		Number of		Number of Inhabitants			
Parishes	Length	Breadth	Parishes	Ministers	Papists	Protestants	Total	Number of Fighting Men
Cleish	4	1	1	1		692	692	138⅖
Kinross	2	2	1	1		1310	1310	262
Orwell	5	2	1	1		1891	1891	378⅕
Portmoak	6	3	1	1		996	996	199⅕
Total			4	4		4889	4889	977⅘
Fife Shire								
Abbotshall	3	3	1	1		1348	1348	269⅗
Abdie	5	2	1	1		822	822	164⅖
Aberdour	4	2	1	1		1198	1198	239⅗
Anstruther Easter	½	1/16	1	1		1100	1100	220
Do. Wester	½	¼	1	1		385	385	77
Auchterderran	4	3	1	1		1143	1143	228⅗
Auchtermuchty	2	1½	1	1		1308	1308	261⅗
Auchtertool	2	1	1	1		389	389	77⅘
Ballingry	3	3	1	1		464	464	92⅘
Balmerino	2½	1	1	1		565	565	113
Carried Over			10	10		8722	8722	1744⅖

Fife Shire	Extent		Number of		Number of Inhabitants			
Parishes	Length	Breadth	Parishes	Ministers	Papists	Protestants	Total	Number of Fighting Men
Brot. Over			10	10		8722	8722	$1744\frac{2}{5}$
Beith	3	2	1	1		1099	1099	$219\frac{4}{5}$
Burnt-island	2	1	1	1		1390	1390	278
Cameron	$4\frac{1}{2}$	3	1	1		1295	1295	259
Carnbee	$3\frac{1}{2}$	3	1	1		1293	1293	$258\frac{3}{5}$
Carnock	$2\frac{1}{2}$	2	1	1		583	583	$116\frac{3}{5}$
Ceres	6	3	1	1		2540	2540	508
Colessie	$4\frac{1}{2}$	$1\frac{1}{2}$	1	1		989	989	$197\frac{4}{5}$
Coupar	$2\frac{3}{4}$	$2\frac{3}{4}$	1	2		2192	2192	$438\frac{2}{5}$
Crail	5	2	1	1		2173	2173	$434\frac{3}{5}$
Creich	$1\frac{1}{2}$	1	1	1		375	375	75
Cult	2	2	1	1		449	449	$89\frac{4}{5}$
Dairsie	2	$1\frac{1}{2}$	1	1		469	469	$93\frac{4}{5}$
Dalgety	3	1	1	1		761	761	$152\frac{1}{5}$
Dennino	2	2	1	1		598	598	$119\frac{3}{5}$
Dunfermline	5	4	1	2		8552	8552	$1710\frac{2}{5}$
Dunboig	$1\frac{1}{2}$	$1\frac{1}{2}$	1	1		255	255	51
Dysert	3	$1\frac{1}{2}$	1	2		2367	2367	$473\frac{2}{5}$
Ely	1	$\frac{1}{2}$	1	1		642	642	$128\frac{2}{5}$
Carried Over			28	31		36744	36744	$7348\frac{4}{5}$

Fife Shire	Extent		Number of		Number of Inhabitants			
PARISHES	Length	Breadth	Parishes	Ministers	Papists	Protestants	Total	Number of Fighting Men
Brot. Over			28	31		36744	36744	$7348\frac{4}{5}$
Falkland	3	2	1	1		1795	1795	359
Ferrypartoncraig	2	$\frac{1}{2}$	1	1		621	621	$124\frac{1}{5}$
Flisk	3	2	1	1		318	318	$63\frac{3}{5}$
Forgan	$3\frac{1}{2}$	1	1	1		751	751	$150\frac{1}{5}$
Inverkeithing	4	2	1	1		1694	1694	$338\frac{4}{5}$
Kemback	$1\frac{1}{3}$	$1\frac{1}{4}$	1	1		420	420	84
Kennoway	1	1	1	1		1240	1240	248
Kettle	5	$1\frac{1}{2}$	1	1		1621	1621	$324\frac{1}{5}$
Kinghorn	$3\frac{1}{2}$	$2\frac{1}{2}$	1	1		2389	2389	$477\frac{4}{5}$
Kinglassie	2	2	1	1		998	998	$199\frac{3}{5}$
Kilconquhar	5	2	1	1		2131	2131	$426\frac{1}{5}$
Kilmany	4	2	1	1		781	781	$156\frac{1}{5}$
Kilrenny	3	2	1	1		1348	1348	$269\frac{3}{5}$
Kingsbarns	2	$1\frac{1}{2}$	1	1		871	871	$174\frac{1}{5}$
Kirkaldy	1	$\frac{1}{2}$	1	1		2296	2296	$459\frac{1}{5}$
Largo	$2\frac{1}{2}$	2	1	1		1396	1396	$279\frac{1}{5}$
Leslie	2	2	1	1		1130	1130	226
Leuchars	6	6	1	1		1691	1691	$338\frac{1}{5}$
Carried Over			46	49		60235	60235	12047

Fife Shire	Extent		Number of		Number of Inhabitants			
Parishes	Length	Breadth	Parishes	Ministers	Papists	Protestants	Total	Number of Fighting Men
Brot. Over			46	49		60235	60235	12047
Logie	2	1¼	1	1		413	413	82⅗
Markinch	4	4	1	1		2188	2188	437⅗
Monymail	3	2	1	1		884	884	176⅘
Moonzie	1	¾	1	1		249	249	49⅘
Newburgh	2	1	1	1		1347	1347	269⅖
Newburn	1¾	1¾	1	1		438	438	87⅗
Pittenweem	¼		1	1		939	939	187⅘
Saline	4	4	1	1		1285	1285	257
Scoonie	2	1	1	1		1528	1528	305⅗
St. Andrews	6	2	1	2	8	4582	4590	918
St. Leonards [1]	3	½	1	1		323	323	64⅗
St. Monance	1	½	1	1		780	780	156
Strathmiglo	5½ 5	1½ 1½	1	1		1695	1695	339
Torryburn	2	2	1	1		1635	1635	327
Weemyss	3½	1	1	1		3041	3041	608⅕
Total			61	65	8	81562	81570	16314

[1] St. Leonards Is not properly a Parish Church but a Chapel of Ease, of which the Principal of St. Leonards College in the University of St. Andrews is Minister Ex officio.

PERTH SHIRE	Extent		Number of		Number of Inhabitants			
PARISHES	Length	Breadth	Parishes	Ministers	Papists	Protestants	Total	Number of Fighting Men
Aberdalgie	2	2	1	1		320	320	64
Aberfoyl	7	6	1	1		895	895	179
Abernethy	3	3	1	1		1490	1490	298
Abernyte	2	$1\frac{1}{2}$	1	1		258	258	$51\frac{3}{5}$
Alyth	12	4	1	1		2680	2680	536
Arngosk	2	2	1	1		736	736	$147\frac{1}{5}$
Auchterarder	4	4	1	1		1194	1194	$238\frac{4}{5}$
Auchtergaven	7	2	1	1		1677	1677	$335\frac{2}{5}$
Balquhidder	11	7	1	1	6	1586	1592	$318\frac{2}{5}$
Blackford	5	5	1	1		1681	1681	$336\frac{1}{5}$
Blair Athol	11	$8\frac{1}{2}$	1	1		3257	3257	$651\frac{2}{5}$
Blairgowrie	8	$2\frac{1}{2}$	1	1		1596	1596	$319\frac{1}{5}$
Bendochy	8	4	1	1		1293	1293	$258\frac{3}{5}$
Callender	20	6	1	1	13	1737	1750	350
Caputh	9	4	1	1	1	2047	2048	$409\frac{3}{5}$
Cargil	5	4	1	1	60	1837	1897	$379\frac{2}{5}$
Clunie	5	5	1	1		905	905	181
Collace	$1\frac{1}{2}$	1	1	1		499	499	$99\frac{4}{5}$
Comrie	10	10	1	1	6	2540	2546	$509\frac{1}{5}$
Carried Over			19	19	86	28228	28314	$5662\frac{4}{5}$

PERTH SHIRE	Extent		Number of		Number of Inhabitants			
PARISHES	Length	Breadth	Parishes	Ministers	Papists	Protestants	Total	Number of Fighting Men
Brot. Over			19	19	86	28228	28314	5662⅘
Coupar [1]	3½	1	1	1	1	1490	1491	298⅕
Crieff [2]	3	3	1	1	3	1411	1414	282⅘
Culross	3	2½	1	2		1695	1695	339
Dron	3	1½	1	1		598	598	119⅗
Dull	22	12	1	1		5748	5748	1149⅗
Dunbarnie	2½	2	1	1		764	764	152⅘
Dunblane	9	4	1	1		2728	2728	545⅗
Dunkeld	8	1	1	1	1	1297	1298	259⅗
Dunkeld Little			1	1	8	2911	2919	583⅘
Dunning	5	3	1	1	1	1490	1491	298⅕
Inchmartine & Errol	4	2	1	1		2229	2229	445⅘
Forgandenny	5	1	1	1		1295	1295	259
Forteviot	8	2	1	1		1164	1164	232⅘
Fortingal	21	8	1	1		3859	3859	771⅘
Fossway	6	6	1	1		1765	1765	353
Fowlis Wester	7	6	1	1		1706	1706	341⅕
Gask	2	1½	1	1		385	385	77
Glendovan	3½	1	1	1		220	220	44
Carried Over			37	38	100	60983	61083	12216⅗

[1] COUPAR—A small part of this Parish lyes in Forfar Shire.

[2] CRIEFF—There is a Glen belongs to this Parish called Glenalmond not included in the Extent stated above which is 3 Miles long and 5 distant from the Church.

PERTH SHIRE	Extent		Number of		Number of Inhabitants			
PARISHES	Length	Breadth	Parishes	Ministers	Papists	Protestants	Total	Number of Fighting Men
Brot. Over			37	38	100	60983	61083	12216 3/5
Inchture	2	2	1	1		893	893	178 3/5
Kenmore	21	5	1	1		3067	3067	613 2/5
Killin	19	3	1	1	5	1963	1968	393 3/5
Kilmadock	12	9	1	1		2730	2730	546
Kilspindie	2	2	1	1		828	828	165 3/5
Kincardin	7	4	1	1	2	1248	1249 1250	250
Kinclavin	3	3	1	1	1	992	994 993	198 3/5
Kinfauns	4	1	1	1		639	639	127 4/5
Kinloch	3	1	1	1		331	331	66 1/5
Kinnaird	3	2	1	1		557	557	111 2/5
Kinnoul	5	5	1	1	1	1162	1163	232 3/5
Kippen	6½	4	1	1		1799	1799	359 4/5
Kirkmichael	11	5	1	1	5	2684	2689	537 4/5
Lecropt	1½	1	1	1		577	577	115 2/5
Lethendie	1	½	1	1		346	346	69 1/5
Logie	4	4	1	1		1985	1985	397
Logierait			1	1	3	2484	2487	497 2/5
Longforgan	6	3	1	1		1285	1285	257
Carried Over			55	56	117	86553	86670	17334

Perth Shire	Extent		Number of		Number of Inhabitants			
Parishes	Length	Breadth	Parishes	Ministers	Papists	Protestants	Total	Number of Fighting Men
Brot. Over			55	56	117	86553	86670	17334
Maderty	3	2	1	1		796	796	159⅕
Meigle	3	1½	1	1		1285	1285	257
Methven	4	3	1	1		1790	1790	358
Monedie	3	2	1	1	1	1491	1492	298⅖
Monivaird	4	4	1	1		1460	1460	292
Monzie	5	4	1	1		1192	1192	238⅖
Moulin	12	8	1	1	2	2017 2107	2109	421⅘
Muckart	3	2	1	1		535	535	107
Muthil	8	8	1	1	59	2843	2902	580⅖
Perth [1]	2	½	1	2	1	9018	9019	1803⅘
Port	7	6	1	1		1865	1865	373
Rattray	3	1½	1	1		751	751	150⅕
Regorton	4	3	1	1	1	1073	1074	214⅘
Rhynd	2	1	1	1		498	498	99⅗
Scone	3	2	1	1	1	888	889	177⅘
St. Madois	1	1	1	1		189	189	37⅘
St. Martins	4	3	1	1	4	1079	1083	216⅗
Tibbermuir	4	1	1	1		988	988	197⅗
Carried Over			73	75	186	116401	116587	23317⅖

[1] Perth—It is believed this Town now contains about 12000 Inhabitants.

PERTH SHIRE	Extent		Number of		Number of Inhabitants			
PARISHES	Length	Breadth	Parishes	Ministers	Papists	Protestants	Total	Number of Fighting Men
Brot. Over			73	75	186	116401	116587	23317⅖
Trinity-Gask	3	1	1	1	8	905	913	182⅗
Tulliallan	2	2	1	1		1321	1321	264⅕
Weem	23	10	1	1		1295	1295	259
Total			76	78	194	119922	120116	24023⅕
FORFAR SHIRE								
Aberbrothwick	1	½	1	1	1	2097	2098	419⅗
Arbirlot	3	1½	1	1		865	865	173
Aberlemno	4	4	1	1		943	943	188⅗
Airly	6	3	1	1		1013	1013	202⅗
Auchterhouse	4	4	1	1		600	600	120
Barrie	3	2	1	1		689	689	137⅘
Benvie	4	2¼	1	1		1311	1311	262⅕
Brechin	5	4	1	2	1	3180	3181	636⅕
Carmylie	4	2	1	1		745	745	149
Carroldstone	1½	1	1	1		269	369	53⅘
Carried Over			10	11	2	11712	11714	2342⅘

FORFAR SHIRE	Extent		Number of		Number of Inhabitants			
PARISHES	Length	Breadth	Parishes	Ministers	Papists	Protestants	Total	Number of Fighting Men
Brot. Over			10	11	2	11712	11714	2342⅘
Cortachie	12	4	1	1	1	1232	1233	246⅗
Craig	2½	1	1	1		935	935	187
Dun	2	1½	1	1		657	657	131⅖
Dundee [1]	4	4	1	5 3	3	12474	12477	2495⅖
Dunnichen	2½	2	1	1		653	653	130⅗
Eassie	2½	¾	1	1		500	500	100
Edzel	8	1½	1	1		862	862	172⅖
Farnwell	4	2	1	1		509	509	101⅘
Fern	4	2	1	1		500	500	100
Forfar	4	4	1	1	3	2447	2450	490
Glammis	8	6	1	1	4	1776	1780	356
Glenyla	11	5½	1	1		1852	1852	370⅖
Guthrie	2	1	1	1		584	584	116⅘
Inverarity	3½	3½	1	1		996	996	199⅕
Inverkeillor	5	2	1	1		1286	1286	257⅕
Kinnaird [2]	2	1	1	1		290	290	58
Kinnel	2½	2	1	1		761	761	152⅕
Kirkden	4½	1½	1	1		585	585	117
Carried Over			28	33	13	40611	40624	8125⅘

[1] DUNDEE—This Town has encreased so considerably that there have been added two Parish Churches to the Establishment in the Course of last year. It is computed the Inhabitants now amount to near 18000.

[2] KINNAIRD—This Parish is now Suppressed and United to the Parishes of Bechin and Farnwell.

FORFAR SHIRE	Extent		Number of		Number of Inhabitants			
PARISHES	Length	Breadth	Parishes	Ministers	Papists	Protestants	Total	Number of Fighting Men
Brot. Over			28	33	13	40611	40624	$8125\frac{4}{5}$
Kettins	$3\frac{1}{2}$	2	1	1		1475	1475	295
Kingoldrum	4	2	1	1		780	780	156
Kinnettles	2	$1\frac{1}{2}$	1	1	8	608	616	$123\frac{1}{5}$
Kirrymuir	11	4	1	1		3409	3409	$681\frac{4}{5}$
Lintrathen	8	5	1	1		1165	1165	233
Lochlee	8	3	1	1	10	676	686	$137\frac{1}{5}$
Logie	4	2	1	1		696	696	$139\frac{1}{5}$
Lunan	1	1	1	1		208	208	$41\frac{3}{5}$
Lundie & Fowlis [1]	7	$3\frac{3}{4}$	1	1		586	586	$117\frac{1}{5}$
Mains	3	2	1	1		709	709	$141\frac{4}{5}$
Maryton	5	2	1	1		633	633	$126\frac{3}{5}$
Menmuir	4	$1\frac{1}{2}$	1	1		743	743	$148\frac{3}{5}$
Monikie	4	4	1	1		1345	1345	269
Monifeith	3	$2\frac{1}{2}$	1	1		1421	1421	$284\frac{1}{5}$
Montrose	2	1	1	2	3	4147	4150	830
Muirhouse	3	$2\frac{1}{2}$	1	1		623	623	$124\frac{3}{5}$
Navar & Lethnot	6	4	1	1		635	635	127
Newtyld	2	2	1	1		913	913	$182\frac{3}{5}$
Carried Over			46	52	34	61303	61417	$12283\frac{2}{5}$

[1] LUNDIE &c.—Part of this Parish lyes in Perth Shire.

Forfar Shire	Extent		Number of		Number of Inhabitants			
Parishes	Length	Breadth	Parishes	Ministers	Papists	Protestants	Total	Number of Fighting Men
Brot. Over			46	52	34	61383	61417	12283⅖
Oathlaw	3	1	1	1		435	435	87
Panbride	4	3	1	1		1259	1259	251⅘
Rescobie	5½	2	1	1	1	797	798	159⅗
Ruthven	2	2	1	1		280	280	56
St. Vigians	6	4	1	1		1592	1592	318⅖
Strathmartine	1½	¾	1	1		368	368	73⅗
Strickathrow	4	1	1	1		529	529	105⅘
Tannadice	7	6	1	1		1470	1470	294
Tealing	4	2	1	1		735	735	147
Total			55	61	35	68848	68883	13776⅗

Kincardin Shire								
Arbuthnot	4	4	1	1		997	997	199⅖
Banchory Devonick [1]	4	3	1	1		1495	1495	299
Banchory Ternan [1]	7	6	1	1	7	1729	1736	347⅕
Benholm	2	1½	1	1		1367	1367	273⅖
Carried Over			4	4	7	5588	5595	1119

[1] Banchory Devonick & Banchory Ternan—Part of these Parishes lye in Aberdeen Shire.

KINCARDIN SHIRE	Extent		Number of		Number of Inhabitants			
PARISHES	Length	Breadth	Parishes	Ministers	Papists	Protestants	Total	Number of Fighting Men
Brot. Over			4	4	7	5588	5595	1119
Bervie	2	1	1	1		655	655	131
Dunnottar	5	3	1	1		1570	1570	314
Durris	5	$2\frac{1}{2}$	1	1		889	889	$177\frac{4}{5}$
Ecclesgreig	4	2	1	1		1271	1271	$254\frac{1}{5}$
Fettercairn	4	2	1	1		1950	1950	390
Fetteresso	9	5	1	1		3082	3082	$616\frac{2}{5}$
Fordun	6	6	1	1		1890	1890	378
Garvock	5	3	1	1		755	755	151
Glenbervie	5	5	1	1		958	958	$191\frac{3}{5}$
Kinneff	$3\frac{1}{2}$	2	1	1		858	858	$171\frac{3}{5}$
Laurencekirk	$3\frac{1}{2}$	$2\frac{1}{2}$	1	1		757	757	$151\frac{2}{5}$
Maryculter	$4\frac{1}{2}$	$2\frac{1}{2}$	1	1	10	736	746	$149\frac{1}{5}$
Marykirk	4	4	1	1		1285	1285	257
Strachan	13	9	1	1		796	796	$159\frac{1}{5}$
Total			18	18	17	23040	23057	$4611\frac{2}{5}$

ABERDEEN SHIRE	Extent		Number of		Number of Inhabitants			
PARISHES	Length	Breadth	Parishes	Ministers	Papists	Protestants	Total	Number of Fighting Men
Aberdeen [1]	1 $\frac{1}{2}$	$\frac{1}{2}$	1	4	135	10353	297 10488 10785	2097$\frac{3}{5}$
Aberdour	6	4$\frac{1}{2}$	1	1		1397	1397	279$\frac{2}{5}$
Aboyne	8	3	1	1	58	1637	1695	339
Alford	4	2	1	1		990	990	198
Auchindore	5	1	1	1		839	839	167$\frac{4}{5}$
Auchterless	5	2	1	1	2	1262	1264	252$\frac{4}{5}$
Belhelvie	4$\frac{1}{2}$	3	1	1		1471	1471	294$\frac{1}{5}$
Birse	6	4	1	1	22	1104	1126	225$\frac{1}{5}$
Bourty	3	1$\frac{1}{2}$	1	1		525	525	105
Cabrach	6	3	1	1	84	876	960	192
Cairny & Ruthven [2]	6$\frac{1}{2}$	3	1	1	400	2290	2690	538
Chapel of Garioch	6	3	1	1	3	1348	1351	270$\frac{1}{5}$
Clatt	2	2	1	1		559	559	111$\frac{4}{5}$
Clunie	6	2	1	1		994	994	198$\frac{4}{5}$
Coull	4	3$\frac{1}{2}$	1	1	3	748	751	150$\frac{1}{5}$
Crathie & Braemar	16	6	1	1	684	1987	2671	534$\frac{1}{5}$
Crimond	4	2	1	1	3	762	765	153
Cruden	5	5	1	1		2549	2549	509$\frac{4}{5}$
Culsalmond	3	3	1	1		810	810	162
Carried Over			19	22	1394	32501	33895	6779

[1] ABERDEEN—From the most authentic Accounts the Inhabitants of this Town including Footdie and Old Machar, now amount to about 22000.

[2] CAIRNY &c.—Part of this Parish lyes in Banff Shire.

Aberdeen Shire	Extent		Number of		Number of Inhabitants			
Parishes	Length	Breadth	Parishes	Ministers	Papists	Protestants	Total	Number of Fighting Men
Brot. Over			19	22	1394	32501	33895	6779
Cushny	3½	2½	1	1		500	500	100
Daviot	2	2	1	1	2	973	975	195
Deer New	10	4	1	1	16	2297	2313	462⅗
Deer Old	9	7	1	1	9	2804	2813	462⅗
Drumblade	4	4	1	1	6	1119	1125	225
Drumoak	3	2	1	1	1	759	760	152
Dyce	4½	2	1	1		383	383	76⅗
Echt	3	2	1	1	1	1276	1277	255⅖
Ellon	6	6	1	1	1	2522	2523	504⅗
Fintry	3	3	1	1	1	904	905	181
Footdie [1]	½	¼	1	1		297	297	59⅖
Forbes	7½	3½	1	1		456	456	91⅕
Forgue	7	3½	1	1	8	1794	1802	360⅖
Foveran	4	3	1	1	1	1980	1981	396⅕
Fraserburgh	6	4	1	1	5	1677	1682	336⅖
Fyvie	9	6	1	1	4	2524	2528	505⅗
Glass [2]	5½	2½	1	1	50	1043	1093	218⅗
Glenbucket	3	1	1	1	5	425	430	86
Carried Over			37	40	1504	56234	57738	11547⅗

[1] Footdie—This is not properly a distinct Parish, but a part of the Parish of Aberdeen; the Erection was about the 1631 by voluntary Contribution.

[2] Glass—Part of this Parish lyes in Banff Shire.

ABERDEEN SHIRE	Extent		Number of		Number of Inhabitants			
PARISHES	Length	Breadth	Parishes	Ministers	Papists	Protestants	Total	Number of Fighting Men
Brot. Over			37	40	1504	56234	57738	11547$\frac{3}{5}$
Glenmuik	12	12	1	1	407	1863	2270	454
Inch	3	2	1	1		995	995	199
Inverury	3	2	1	1		730	730	146
Keig	2	2	1	1	1	498	499	99$\frac{4}{5}$
Keithhall	4	2	1	1		825	825	165
Kemnay	4	1$\frac{1}{2}$	1	1		643	643	128$\frac{3}{5}$
Kincardin Oneil	5$\frac{1}{2}$	5	1	1	6	1700	1706	341$\frac{1}{5}$
Kildrummy	4	3	1	1	2	560	562	112$\frac{2}{5}$
King Edward	9	2	1	1	13	1339	1352	270$\frac{2}{5}$
Kinkell [1]	3	2	1	1		429	429	85$\frac{4}{5}$
Kinnellar	2$\frac{1}{2}$	1	1	1		398	398	79$\frac{3}{5}$
Kinnethmont	4	1	1	1	8	783	791	158$\frac{1}{5}$
Kintore	3	2	1	1		830	830	166
Leochel	3$\frac{1}{2}$	2	1	1	1	785	786	157$\frac{1}{5}$
Lesly	1$\frac{1}{2}$	1	1	1		319	319	63$\frac{4}{5}$
Logie Buchan	7	1$\frac{1}{2}$	1	1		575	575	115
Logie Colstone	6	3	1	1	2	1241	1243	248$\frac{3}{5}$
Longmay	7	2	1	1		1674	1674	334$\frac{4}{5}$
Carried Over			55	58	1944	72421	74365	14873

[1] KINKELL—This Parish is now Suppressed and annexed to Keithhall.

Aberdeen Shire	Extent		Number of		Number of Inhabitants			
Parishes	Length	Breadth	Parishes	Ministers	Papists	Protestants	Total	Number of Fighting Men
Brot. Over			55	58	1944	72421	74365	14873
Longside	4	4	1	1	5	1974	1979	395 4/5
Lumphanan	4	4	1	1	9	673	682	136 2/5
Methlick	4½	4½	1	1		1385	1385	277
Midmar	4	2	1	1		979	979	185 4/5
Monwhitter			1	1	5	992	997	199 2/5
Monymusk	3½	2	1	1		1005	1005	201
Newhills	4½	4½	1	1		959	959	191 4/5
New Machar	6	1	1	1		1191	1191	238 1/5
Nigg	3	2	1	1		1289	1289	257 4/5
Old Machar or Old Aberdeen	5	1½	1	2	58	4887	4945	989
Old Meldrum	3	1½	1	1	1	1602	1603	320 3/5
Oyne	5	3	1	1		643	643	128 3/5
Peterculter	3½	3½	1	1	2	753	755	151
Peterhead	4	2½	1	1		2487	2487	497 2/5
Pitsligo	3	2	1	1		1224	1224	244 4/5
Premnay	2	2	1	1		448	448	89 3/5
Rathen	5	3	1	1	7	1520	1527	305 2/5
Rayne	2	2	1	1		1131	1131	226 1/5
Carried Over			73	77	2031	97563	99594	19918 4/5

ABERDEEN SHIRE	Extent		Number of		Number of Inhabitants			
PARISHES	Length	Breadth	Parishes	Ministers	Papists	Protestants	Total	Number of Fighting Men
Brot. Over			73	77	2031	97563	99594	19918$\frac{4}{5}$
Rhynie	6	3	1	1	8	828	836	167$\frac{1}{5}$
St. Fergus	5	3	1	1		1271	1271	254$\frac{1}{5}$
Skene	4	1$\frac{1}{2}$	1	1	2	1249	1251	250$\frac{1}{5}$
Slains	4	3	1	1		1286	1286	257$\frac{1}{5}$
Strathdon	12	4	1	1	190	1560	1750	350
Strichen	4	2	1	1	1	1157	1158	231$\frac{3}{5}$
Tarland	12$\frac{1}{2}$		1	1	40	1260	1300	260
Tarves	6	5$\frac{1}{2}$	1	1	2	2344	2346	469$\frac{1}{5}$
Tillynessle	3	1	1	1		335	335	67
Tough	3$\frac{1}{2}$	2	1	1		570	570	114
Towie	4	3	1	1	2	654	656	131$\frac{1}{5}$
Turriff	6	2	1	1	11	1886	1897	379$\frac{3}{5}$
Tyrie	5$\frac{1}{2}$	2	1	1	1	595	596	119$\frac{1}{5}$
Udny	5	5	1	1		1322	1322	264$\frac{2}{5}$
Total			87	91	2288	113880	116168	23233$\frac{3}{5}$

Banff Shire	Extent		Number of		Number of Inhabitants			
Parishes	Length	Breadth	Parishes	Ministers	Papists	Protestants	Total	Number of Fighting Men
Aberlour	5½	3½	1	1	24	986	1010	202
Alvah	5	3	1	1	2	1159	1161	232⅕
Banff	4	1	1	1	6	2994	3000	600
Bellie	7	3	1	1	540	1190	1730	346
Boharm	2½	½	1	1	2	833	835	167
Botriphny	2½	1½	1	1	7	946	953	190⅗
Boyndie	4	2	1	1		994	994	189⅘ 198⅘
Cullen	1	½	1	1		900	900	180
Deskford	2½	2	1	1	1	939	940	188
Forglen	3½	3	1	1	1	606	607	121⅖
Fordice	4	3	1	1	2	3210	3212	642⅖
Gamery	8	4	1	1		2083	2083	416⅗
Gartley	6	2	1	1	11	1317	1328	265⅗
Grainge	5	3	1	1	62	1735	1797	359⅖
Huntly	6	2	1	1	233	1667	1900	380
Inneraven	9	3	1	1	843	1621	2464	492⅘
Inverkeithny	3	2	1	1		571	571	114⅕
Keith	4	4	1	1	30	2653	2683	536⅗
Kirkmichael	10	3	1	1	431	857	1288	257⅗
Carried Over			19	19	2195	27261	29456	5891⅕

BANFF SHIRE	Extent		Number of		Number of Inhabitants			
PARISHES	Length	Breadth	Parishes	Ministers	Papists	Protestants	Total	Number of Fighting Men
Brot. Over			19	19	2195	27261	29456	5891⅕
Marnock	6	3	1	1	20	1874	1894	474⅘ 378⅘
Mortlich	6½	6½	1	1	75	2299	2374	378⅘ 474⅘
Ordequhil	2	1½	1	1	3	663	666	133⅕
Rathven	7	4	1	1	822	2076	2898	579⅗
Rothemay	5	4	1	1	35	1155	1190	238
Total			24	24	3150	35328	38478	7695⅗
SHIRE OF ELGIN & MORAY								
Abernethy [1]	10	5	1	1	8	1662	1670	334
Alves	4	2	1	1		1691	1691	338⅕
Birnie	3	1	1	1		525	525	105
Dollas	5	4	1	1	1	699	700	140
Drainie	4	2	1	1		1174	1174	234⅘
Duffus	3½	2	1	1		1679	1679	335⅘
Dundurcus	5	2	1	1	5	1189	1194	238⅘
Carried Over			7	7	14	8619	8633	1726⅗

[1] ABERNETHY—Part of this Parish lyes in Inverness Shire.

G

Elgin Shire	Extent		Number of		Number of Inhabitants			
Parishes	Length	Breadth	Parishes	Ministers	Papists	Protestants	Total	Number of Fighting Men
Brot. Over			7	7	14	8619	8633	726⅗
Duthill & Rothemurcus [1]	10	7	1	1	25	1760	1785	357
Dyke	5	2	1	1	1	1825	1826	365⅕
Eddinkillie	9	3	1	1	3	1440	1443	288⅗
Elgin	8	3½	1	2	12	6294	6306	1261⅕
Forres	3	2	1	1		1993	1993	398⅗
Kinloss	3	3	1	1		1191	1191	238⅕
Knockando	6	2	1	1	3	1264	1267	253⅖
Longbride [2]	1½	11	1	1		442	442	88⅖
New Speynie	3½	3	1	1		865	865	173
Rafford	5	4	1	1		1313	1313	262⅗
Rothes	4½	3	1	1	2	744	746	149⅕
St. Andrews	3	3	1	1		690	690	138
Speymouth	3½	1	1	1	30	964	994	198⅘
Urquhart	3	2	1	1		1110	1110	222
Total			21	22	90	30514	30604	6120⅘

[1] Duthill & Rothemurcus—Rothemurcus which is but a small part of the United Parish is in Inverness Shire.

[2] Longbride—This Parish is now Suppressed and United to the Parish of St. Andrews.

NAIRN SHIRE	Extent		Number of		Number of Inhabitants			
PARISHES	Length	Breadth	Parishes	Ministers	Papists	Protestants	Total	Number of Fighting Men
Ardclaugh	8	7	1	1		1163	1163	232$\frac{3}{5}$
Auldearn	5	5	1	1		1951	1951	390$\frac{1}{5}$
Calder [1]	4	4	1	1		882	882	176$\frac{2}{5}$
Nairn	4	3$\frac{1}{2}$	1	1		1698	1698	339$\frac{3}{5}$
Total			4	4		5694	5694	1138$\frac{4}{5}$
INVERNESS SHIRE								
Alvie	7	6$\frac{1}{2}$	1	1	2	1019	1021	204$\frac{1}{5}$
Barra			1	1	1100	50	1150	230
Boleskine	18	17	1	1	428	1533	1961	392$\frac{1}{5}$
Braccadale	14	8	1	1		1907	1907	381$\frac{2}{5}$
Cromdale	12	6	1	1	2	3061	3063	612$\frac{3}{5}$
Croy	12 12	12 2	1	1		1901	1901	380$\frac{1}{5}$
Daviot	15	4	1	1	45	2131	2176	435$\frac{1}{5}$
Dores	13	3	1	1	12	1508	1520	304
Duirnish	15	15 8	1	1		2568	2568	513$\frac{3}{5}$
Glenelg	36	20	1	1	827	989	1816	363$\frac{1}{5}$
Carried Over			10	10	2416	16667	19083	3816$\frac{3}{5}$

[1] CALDER—Part of this Parish lyes in Inverness Shire.

INVERNESS SHIRE	Extent		Number of		Number of Inhabitants			
PARISHES	Length	Breadth	Parishes	Ministers	Papists	Protestants	Total	Number of Fighting Men
Brot. Over			10	10	2416	16667	19083	3816⅗
Harris	24	12	1	1		1969	1969	393⅘
Inverness	9	2	1	3		9730	9730	1946
Kilmalie [1]	37	25	1	1	20	3073	3093	618⅗
Kilmorak	32	12	1	1	564	2266	2830	566
Kilmuir	12	4	1	1		1572	1572	314⅖
Kiltarlity	18	4	1	1	402	1562	1964	392⅘
Kinguissie	11	6	1	1	2	1898	1900	380
Kirkhill	4	2½	1	1		1360	1360	272
Laggan	18	16	1	1	130	1330	1460	292
Moy	14	4	1	1	1	1692	1693	338⅗
North Uist	18	12	1	1		1909	1909	381⅘
Petty	5½	1	1	1		1643	1643	328⅗
Portree	7	4	1	1		1385	1385	277
Slate	12	2½	1	1		1250	1250	250
Snizort	10	8	1	1		1627	1627	325⅖
South Uist & Benbicula	30	7	1	1	2040	169	2209	441⅘
Strath	13	4	1	1		943	943	188⅗
Urquhart	18	12	1	1	89	1854	1943	388⅗
Total			28	30	5664	53899	59563	11912⅗

[1] KILMALIE—Part of this Parish lyes in Argyle Shire.

Ross Shire	Extent		Number of		Number of Inhabitants			
PARISHES	Length	Breadth	Parishes	Ministers	Papists	Protestants	Total	Number of Fighting Men
Alness	12	5	1	1		1090	1090	218
Applecross	26	12	1	1		835	835	167
Ardersier	3	1½	1	1		428	428	85⅗
Avoch	2	2	1	1		1457	1457	291⅖
Barvas	16		1	1		1995	1995	399
Contin [1]	19	17	1	1	2	1947	1949	389⅘
Dingwall	5	2	1	1	1	1029	1030	206
Edderton	7	2½	1	1		780	780	156
Fearn [1]	3	2½	1	1		1898	1898	379⅗
Gairloch	30	18	1	1	1	2049	2050	410
Glenshiel	16	4	1	1	7	502	509	101⅘
Kilernan	1½	1	1	1		945	945	189
Kilmuir Easter [1]			1	1		1095	1095	219
Kilmuir Wester	3½	2	1	1		660	699 668 1367	133⅗
Kiltearn	7	4	1	1		1570	1570	314
Kincardin [1]	20	13	1	1		1743	1743	348⅗
Kintail	16	13	1	1	3	695	698	139⅗
Kirkmichael [1]	5	2	1	1		1371	1371	274⅕
Lochalsh	20	4	1	1		613	613	122⅗
Carried Over			19	19	14	22710	22724	4544⅘

[1] CONTIN, FEARN, KILMUIR EASTER, KINCARDIN & KIRKMICHAEL—Part of these Parishes lye in Cromarty Shire.

Ross Shire	Extent		Number of		Number of Inhabitants			
Parishes	Length	Breadth	Parishes	Ministers	Papists	Protestants	Total	Number of Fighting Men
Brot. Over			19	19	14	22710	22724	$4544\frac{4}{5}$
Lochbroom [1]	36	20	1	1		2211	2211	$442\frac{1}{5}$
Lochcarron	11	7	1	1		771	771	$154\frac{1}{5}$
Lochs	27	10	1	1		1267	1267	$253\frac{2}{5}$
Logie Easter [1]	5	4	1	1		850	850	170
Nigg	3	2	1	1		1261	1261	$252\frac{1}{5}$
Rosekeen	8	3	1	1		1958	1958	$391\frac{3}{5}$
Rosemarkie	5	3	1	1	1	1139	1140	228
Stornoway	17	12	1	1	3	1809	1812	$362\frac{2}{5}$
Suddie	2	1	1	1		699	699	$139\frac{4}{5}$
Tain	6	1	1	1		1870	1870	374
Uigg	22	14	1	1		1312	1312	$262\frac{2}{5}$
Urquhart or Ferntosh [2]	6	2	1	1		2590	2590	518
Urray	7	5	1	1	2	2454	2454 6	$491\frac{1}{5}$
Total			32	32	20	42901	42921	$8584\frac{1}{5}$

[1] Lochbroom, Logie Easter—Part of these Parishes lye in Cromarty Shire.
[2] Urquhart—Part of this Parish lyes in Nairn Shire.

SUTHERLAND SHIRE	Extent		Number of		Number of Inhabitants			
PARISHES	Length	Breadth	Parishes	Ministers	Papists	Protestants	Total	Number of Fighting Men
Assint	20	8	1	1		1934	1934	$386\frac{4}{5}$
Clyne	12	8	1	1		1406	1406	$281\frac{1}{5}$
Creich	24	2	1	1		1705	1705	341
Durness	15	8	1	1		1000	1000	200
Dornoch	9	6	1	1		2780	2780	556
Edderachilis	25	7	1	1		869	869	$173\frac{4}{5}$
Farr	30	12	1	1		2800	2800	560
Golspie	$5\frac{1}{2}$	2	1	1		1790	1790	358
Kildonan	20	10	1	1		1433	1433	$286\frac{3}{5}$
Lairg	18	7	1	1		1010	1010	202
Loth	8	$\frac{1}{2}$	1	1		1193	1193	$238\frac{3}{5}$
Rogart	6	5	1	1		1761	1761	$352\frac{1}{5}$
Tongue	10	8	1	1		1093	1093	$218\frac{3}{5}$
Total			13	13		20774	20774	$4151\frac{4}{5}$
CROMARTY SHIRE								
Cromarty	4	2	1	1	6	2090	2096	$419\frac{1}{5}$
Tarbet [1]	5	2	1	1		1584	1584	$316\frac{4}{5}$
Carried Over			2	2	6	3674	3680	736

[1] TARBET—Part of this Parish lyes in Ross Shire.

CROMARTY SHIRE	Extent		Number of		Number of Inhabitants			
PARISHES	Length	Breadth	Parishes	Ministers	Papists	Protestants	Total	Number of Fighting Men
Brot. Over			2	2	6	3674	3680	736
Fodderty [1]	12	4	1	1	3	1480	1483	296⅗
Total			3	3	9	5154	5163	1032⅗
CAITHNESS SHIRE								
Bower	6½	2½	1	1		1287	1287	257⅖
Canisbay	7	6	1	1		1481	1481	296⅕
Dunnot	2½	2	1	1		1235	1235	247
Halkirk	20	6	1	1		3075	3075	615
Latheron	17	4	1	1		3675	3675	735
Olrigg	3	2	1	1		875	875	175
Reay [2]	21	8	1	1		2262	2262	452⅖
Thurso	6	5	1	1		2963	2963	592⅗
Wattin	6	4	1	1		1424	1424	284⅘
Wick	13½	4	1	1		3938	3938	787⅗
Total			10	10		22215	22215	4443

[1] FODDERTY—Part of this Parish lyes in Ross Shire.

[2] REAY—Part of this Parish lyes in Sutherland Shire.

Orkney Shire	Extent		Number of		Number of Inhabitants			
Parishes	Length	Breadth	Parishes	Ministers	Papists	Protestants	Total	Number of Fighting Men
Bressay & Burray	16	2	1	1		1098	1098	219⅗
Cross Burness & North Ronaldshay	12½	1½	1	1		1250	1250	250
Deerness & St. Andrews	7	3	1	1		1650	1650	330
Delting South & North	11	8	1	1		1221	1221	244⅕
Dunrossness &c.	14	4	1	1		2295	2295	459
Evie & Rendal	7½	3	1	1		1798	1798	359⅗
Fetlar & North Yell	12	9	1	1		1098	1098	219⅗
Firth & Stenness	7	5	1	1		1108	1108	221⅗
Harra & Birsa	9	8	1	1		2200	2200	440
Holm	4	1	1	1		1185	1185	237
Hoy & Gramsay	5	3	1	1		520	520	104
Kirkwall	4	2	1	2		1989	1989	397⅘
Lady Parish	5	1	1	1		750	750	150
Lerwick	4	1	1	1		1193	1193	238⅗
Nesting &c.	16	3	1	1		1169	1169	233⅘
Northmaving	15	8	1	1		1009	1009	201⅘
Orphir [1]	4	2	1	1		855	855	171
Rousay & Egilshay	7½	6	1	1		978	978	195⅗
Sandsting & Aithsting	9	7	1	1		911	911	182⅕
Carried Over			19	20		24277	24277	4855⅖

[1] Orphir—There is an Island Inhabited by Four or Five Families belonging to this Parish One Mile Long & a half Mile Broad—3 Miles distant from the Mainland.

ORKNEY SHIRE	Extent		Number of		Number of Inhabitants			
PARISHES	Length	Breadth	Parishes	Ministers	Papists	Protestants	Total	Number of Fighting Men
Brot. Over			19	20		24277	24277	$4855\frac{2}{5}$
Shapinsay	5	2	1	1		642	642	$128\frac{2}{5}$
South & Mid Yell	9	$5\frac{1}{2}$	1	1		986	986	$197\frac{1}{5}$
South Ronaldsay &c.			1	1		1996	1996	$399\frac{1}{5}$
Stromness & Sand-wicks	8	3	1	1		2677	2677	$535\frac{2}{5}$
Stronsay & Edday	6	$5\frac{1}{2}$	1	1		1493	1493	$298\frac{3}{5}$
Tingwall &c.	10	5	1	1		1412	1412	$282\frac{2}{5}$
Unst	8	3	1	1		1368	1368	$273\frac{3}{5}$
Walls & Flotta &c.			1	1		1000	1000	200
Walls & Sandness &c.	24	12	1	1		1450	1450	290
Westray & Papa Westray	9	$2\frac{1}{2}$	1	1		1290	1290	258
Total			29	30		38591	38591	$7718\frac{1}{5}$

ABSTRACT

of the

preceding List Shewing

The **EXTENT** of each **SHIRE** or **COUNTY** in
measured **MILES**, with the several **COUNTRIES**
and **STRATHS** Comprehended in it.

		Abstract	Extent in
No.	SHIRES	Countrys &c. compre-hended in each	From North to South

			Miles
1	BERWICK	Part of Lawder & of Lamermuir Contains Merse or March	From Dunglass to Coldstream	21
2	HADINGTON	East Lothian	North Berwick to the Head of Gifford Water	19
3	EDINBURGH	Mid Lothian	Musselburgh to the Stow	19½
4	LINLITHGOW	West Lothian	Blackness to the head of Mousewater	17½
5	PEEBLES	Tweedale	Newhall near Linton, to the Loch of the Lows	22
6	SELKIRK	The Forrest of Et-terick	Head of Douglas Water to Loch Elmore	12
7	ROXBURGH	Teviotdale & Lidis-dale	Melrose to the foot of the Water of Liddle	38
8	DUMFRIES	Annandale ; Nithsdale Eskdale and Eusdale	Erickstane Braehead to Annan	32
9	KIRKCUDBRIGHT	A Stewartry and con-tains the East part of Galloway	Waterhead in Cars-phairn to Abbay-head near Kirkcud-bright	40
	Carried Over		

English Miles		Number of		Number of Inhabitants			
From East to West		Parishes	Ministers	Papists	Protestants	Total	Number of Fighting Men
	Miles						
From Berwick to Channelkirk	$25\frac{1}{2}$	32	32		23987	23987	$4797\frac{2}{5}$
Dunglass to Musselburgh	27	24 25	25 26	2	29707	29709	$5941\frac{4}{5}$
Soutra Hill to West Calder	25	40 39	49	263	90149	90412	$18082\frac{2}{5}$
Kirkliston to the foot of Avon Water	$11\frac{1}{2}$	13	14		16829	16829	$3365\frac{4}{5}$
Holylee on Tweed to Biggar	21	16	16	22	8886	8908	$1781\frac{3}{5}$
Foot of Gala Water to Loch Skeen	23	4	4		4021	4021	$804\frac{1}{5}$
Head of Coquet Water to Loch Elmore head of Ale Water	27	35	35		34704	34704	$6940\frac{4}{5}$
Head of Glencairn Water to the head of Euse Water	42	40	41	35	39753	39788	$7957\frac{3}{5}$
Dumfries to Minnigaff	33	28	28	349	20856	21205	4241
		232	244	671	268892	269563	$53912\frac{3}{5}$

		Abstract	Extent in
No.	SHIRES	Countrys &c. comprehended in each	From North to South

				Miles
	Brought Over			
10	WIGTOWN	Contains the West part of Galloway	From Head of Menach Water to Burrowhead	36
11	AIR	The Bailliaries of Kyle, Cunninghame, and Carrick	Kelly to the head of Courin Lane near Lochdoon	56
12	LANERK	the Up Mid & Lower Wards of Clydsdale	Calder on the Water of Kelvin to Queensberryhill	51
13	RENFREW	The Barony of Renfrew	Innerkipp to Cladingraw, head of South Cart Water	28
14	BUTE	The Isles of Bute & Arran	Bute Arran	15½ 26
15	ARGYLE [1]	Argyle, Lorn, Kintyre and Cowell, with the Islands of Islay, Jura, Mull, Lismore Tiree Coll Gigha &c.	Fort William to the Mull of Kintyre	106
16	DUMBARTON	Lennox	Ben Oss, head of Loch Lomond to Dumbarton	31
17	STIRLING	Lyes on both sides of the Forth	Stirling to Kirkintilloch	16
	Carried Over			

[1] ARGYLE—The Extent of this Shire stated above is exclusive of the Islands

English Miles		Number of		Number of Inhabitants			
From East to West		Parishes	Ministers	Papists	Protestants	Total	Number of Fighting Men
	Miles						
		232	244	671	268892	269563	53912⅗
From Port Patrick to Newton Stewart	26	17	17		16466	16466	3293⅕
Eshaw near Muirkirk to Air	26	46 45	48 47		59009	59009	11801⅘
Ingiston Briggs to the head of Avon Water	31	49 46	51 48	2	81724	81726	16345⅕
Renfrew to the Loch of Kilbirnie	13	19	22 21	3	26642	26645	5329
Bute Arran	6 14	5	5		7125	7125	1425
Head of Loch Long to the Port of Craignish	34	39 37	39	4329	61957	66286	13257⅕
Drumtian near Drymen, to Portincaple on Loch Long	18	12	12		13857	13857	2771⅖
Foot of Avon to Bucklyvie	24	21	22	8	37006	37014	7402⅘
		440	460	5013	572678	577691	115538⅕

of Mull, Tiree, Coll, Lesmore &c.

		Abstract	Extent in	
No.	SHIRES	Countrys &c. comprehended in each	From North to South	
				Miles
	Brought Over			
18	CLACKMANAN	Contains a part of the West Corner of Fife	From Head of Devon Water to Alloa	7
19	KINROSS	Part of Fife lying between Loch Leven and the Ochil Hills	Tennant to Loch Orr	8
20	FIFE	The Country of Fife excepting as above	Newburgh to Leven	15
21	PERTH	The Countrys of Gowrie, Athol Glenshee, Strathardel, Breadalbine Glenurchy, Rannach & the Stewartrys of Monteith and Strathern	Head of Glenbrewer to Newburgh on Tay	50
22	FORFAR	Angus with its pertinents as Glenisla, Glenprossin and Glenesk &c.	Head of Glenisla to Button-ness	37
23	ABERDEEN	Marr with its pertinents as Birse, Glentanner, Glenmuik, Strathdee, Strathdon, Brae of Marr, Cromar, Garioch and Strathbogie with most part of Buchan	Banff to Aberdeen	39
24	KINCARDIN	The Mearns	The Kirk of Dores to the foot of North Esk	21
	Carried Over			

ENGLISH MILES		Number of		Number of Inhabitants			
From East to West	Miles	Parishes	Ministers	Papists	Protestants	Total	Number of Fighting Men
		440	460	5013	572678	577691	115538$\frac{1}{2}$
From Kirk of Dollar to foot of Teith Water	12	4	4	2	9001	9003	1800$\frac{3}{5}$
East end of Loch Leven to the Crook of Devon	9	4	4		4889	4889	977$\frac{4}{5}$
St. Andrews to Culross	37	61	65 66	8	81562	81570	16314
Newburgh to Tiendrom	58	76	78	194	119922	120116	24023$\frac{1}{5}$
Foot of N. Esk to Innergowrie	32	55	61 59	35	68848	68883	13776$\frac{3}{5}$
Aberdeen to Head of Dee	73	87	91	2288	113800	116168	23233$\frac{3}{5}$
Stonehaven to Cairnymount	14	18	18	17	23040	23057	4611$\frac{2}{5}$
		745	781	7557	993820	1001377	200275$\frac{2}{5}$

H

		Abstract	Extent in

No.	SHIRES	Countrys &c. compre-hended in each	From North to South	
				Miles
	Brought Over			
25	BANFF	Contains Strathdov-ern, Boyn Enzie Strathaven, Mort-lach, Balveny and a small part of Buchan	From Speymouth to Pitlaw	12½
26	ELGIN & MORAY	The East part of the County of Moray	Foot of Findon to Inveraven	20
27	NAIRN	A small part of the West of Moray	Ardersier to Calder	7
28	INVERNESS [1]	The Countrys of Bad-enoch and Loch-aber; the last of which contains Knoidart, Arisaig, Moidart, Ardna-murchan, Morvern all lying on the West Coast; Loch-arkaig, Locheil, and Swinart; the Islands of South and North Uist, Benbicula Skye &c.	Lochmonnar to Loch-treag	46
29	ROSS [2]	The Country of Ross with the Island of Lewis	The Head of Loch-shinn to the head of Beauly Firth	56
30	CROMARTY [3]	A small part of Ross, south of Cromarty Firth, with the rest of the Earl of Crom-arty's Estate	Kellin to Kirkmichael	10
	Carried Over			

[1] INVERNESS—The Extent of this Shire stated above is exclusive of the Island

[2] ROSS—The Extent of this Shire is exclusive of the Isle of Lewis, which in

[3] CROMARTY—The Extent of this Shire is exclusive of those parts of the late

English Miles		Number of		Number of Inhabitants			
From East to West		Parishes	Ministers	Papists	Protestants	Total	Number of Fighting Men
	Miles						
		745	781	7557	993820	1001377	200275⅖
From Banff to Loch-awin	60	24	24	3150	35328	38478	7695⅗
Speymouth to Head of Findhorn	56	21	22	90	30514	30604	6120⅘
Nairn to Calder	6	4	4		5694	5694	1138⅘
Inverness to the point of Ardnamurchan	100	28	30	5664	53899	59563	11912⅗
Mouth of Cromarty Firth to Applecross Bay	72	32	32	20	42901	42921	8584⅕
The Sutors of Cromarty to Urquhart Castle	12	3	3	9	5154	5163	1032⅗
		857	896	16490	1167310	1183800	236760

of Sky which is about 70 Miles in Length, in some places 30 and in others 40 Miles broad.
Length from the Butt of Lewis to Loch Seaforth is about 60 Miles, and in Breadth from Stornoway to Delmoor about 24 Miles.
Earl of Cromarty's Estate which lye on West Coast.

		Abstract	Extent in
No.	SHIRES	Countrys &c. comprehended in each	From North to South

				Miles
	Brought Over			
31	SUTHERLAND	Contains Sutherland & Strathnaver	From Strathyhead to Dornoch	56
32	CAITHNESS	Caithness	Brimness to the Ord head	28
33	ORKNEY [1]	The Islands of Orkney & Zetland	The Isles of Orkney The Isles of Zetland	70 66
			TOTAL	

[1] ORKNEY—The Extent of the Islands of Orkney above stated, comprehends

ENGLISH MILES		Number of		Number of Inhabitants			
From East to West		Parishes	Ministers	Papists	Protestants	Total	Number of Fighting Men
	Miles						
		857	896	16490	1167310	1183800	236760
From Lochshelly to Lochlaxford	45	13	13		20774	20774	4154⅘
Wick to Loch Garioch	24	10	10		22215	22215	4443
The Isles of Orkney The Isles of Zetland	38 27	29	30		38591	38591	7718½
		909	949	16490	1248890	1265380	253076

the Arms of the Sea which divides them ; the same remark is to be applied to Zetland.

TABLE

shewing

the **NUMBER** of **PEOPLE** in **SCOTLAND** of **ALL AGES**, from the **BIRTH** to the **UTMOST EXTENT OF LIFE.**

In the Year

One thousand Seven hundred and Fifty Five.

EXPLANATION

IT appears from the preceding Abstract, that the Number of People in Scotland amount to 1,265,380 and it has already been observed that the Author received Accounts from a great many Ministers in different parts of the Country, containing not only the number of Souls in their Parishes, but their respective Ages. From these Accounts taken at a Medium, and the Bills of Mortality in Edinburgh Glasgow &c. He calculated the sundry ages of the whole inhabitants as stated in the following Table. The 1st, 3rd, 5th, 7th and 9th Columns shew the Ages; the 2nd, 4th, 6th, 8th and 10th the number of Persons of that Age.

This Table might serve several purposes particularly for Calculating the probabilities of Life and consequently for estimating the value of Annuities in Scotland with more exactness than any Tables yet Extant.

The Tables chiefly in use are founded either on the Births and Burials in London or Breslaw, the Capital City of Silesia, which can be no just Rules in Scotland; Because by comparing these with the following Table, it appears that the generality of People in Scotland live to a greater Age than at London, and not to so great an Age as at Breslaw.[1] But passing over the various uses to which the Adjoined Table may be applied it is sufficient for the Authors present design to say that it affords a good Rule for Calculating the proportion of Men able to bear Arms throughout Scotland in General and every Parish in particular, as was observed in the Introduction to the List of Inhabitants.

---

[1] At Breslaw, One half of the People who are Born live till they are Sixteen years of age, and One fourth of them till 53 years. In Scotland the one half that are Born live only till Eleven years of Age, and the One Fourth of them till 48 years. At London according to some Tables, the one half die before they arrive at the Age of Eight years, and One fourth of them before the Age of 43 years; And according to other Tables they die much sooner, which must necessarily make a considerable alteration in the Chances of Life and consequently in Estimating the value of Annuities.

TABLE SHEWING THE NUMBER OF PEOPLE OF ALL

Age	Persons	Age	Persons	Age	Persons
Under 1	48910	20	22687	40	15758
1	34685	21	22438	41	15345
2	30329	22	22148	42	14916
3	28235	23	21868	43	14487
4	27177	24	21588	44	14074
5	26529	25	21284	45	13661
6	26011	26	20960	46	13248
7	25600	27	20636	47	12835
8	25256	28	20312	48	12456
9	24954	29	19967	49	12045
10	24695	30	19600	50	11634
11	24436	31	19233	51	11223
12	24220	32	18866	52	10812
13	24025	33	18499	53	10401
14	23853	34	18111	54	10016
15	23681	35	17723	55	9649
16	23509	36	17335	56	9282
17	23337	37	16947	57	8915
18	23140	38	16559	58	8548
19	22925	39	16171	59	8181

AGES IN SCOTLAND

Age	Persons	Age	Persons	ABSTRACT [1]	
				Age	Persons
60	7813	80	1359		
61	7446	81	1165	10	322381
62	7101	82	992	20	235813
63	6756	83	863	30	210791
64	6411	84	767	40	175202
65	6066	85	670	50	134701
66	5721	86	574	60	94840
67	5376	87	478	70	58911
68	5031	88	403	80	25659
69	4686	89	328	90	6495
70	4317	90	255	100	587
71	3971	91	202	TOTAL	1265380
72	3625	92	169		
73	3279	93	115		
74	2957	94	72		
75	2655	95			
76	2353				
77	2072		29		
78	1813				
79	1575	100			

[1] In this Abstract the Number of Persons stated in a Line with the Age of 10, include all who are 10 years of Age and under it; Those stated in a Line with the Age of 20, include all who are above 10 and under 21 years of Age, and so on. Those stated in a Line with the Age of 100, include all who are above 90.

POPULATION of SCOTLAND and of the

COUNTIES	BOTH SEXES		
	Webster 1755	1801	1811
SCOTLAND . . .	1,265,380	1,608,420	1,805,864
1. Aberdeen . . .	116,168	121,065	133,871
2. Angus . . .	68,883	99,053	107,187
3. Argyll . . .	66,286	81,277	86,541
4. Ayr . . .	59,009	84,207	103,839
5. Banff . . .	38,478	37,216	38,433
6. Berwick . . .	23,987	30,206	30,893
7. Bute . . .	7,125	11,791	12,033
8. Caithness . . .	22,215	22,609	23,149
9. Clackmannan . .	9,003	10,858	12,010
10. Dumfries . . .	39,788	54,597	62,960
11. Dunbarton . .	13,857	20,710	24,189
12. East Lothian . .	29,709	29,986	31,050
13. Fife	81,570	93,743	101,272
14. Inverness . . .	59,563	72,672	77,671
15. Kincardine . .	23,057	26,349	27,439
16. Kinross . . .	4,889	6,725	7,245
17. Kirkcudbright . .	21,205	29,211	33,684
18. Lanark . . .	81,726	147,692	191,291
19. Midlothian . .	90,412	122,597	148,607
20. Moray . . .	30,604	27,760	27,967
21. Nairn . . .	5,694	8,322	8,496
22. Orkney . . .	23,381	24,445	23,238
23. Peebles . . .	8,908	8,735	9,935
24. Perth . . .	120,116	125,583	134,390
25. Renfrew . . .	26,645	78,501	93,172
26. Ross and Cromarty .	48,084	56,318	60,853
27. Roxburgh . . .	34,704	33,721	37,230
28. Selkirk . . .	4,021	5,388	5,889
29. Stirling . . .	37,014	50,825	58,174
30. Sutherland . .	20,774	23,117	23,629
31. West Lothian . .	16,829	17,844	19,451
32. Wigtown . . .	16,466	22,918	26,891
33. Zetland . . .	15,210	22,379	22,915

NOTE.—The above numbers include the Military in 1841, and both Waters in 1851, 1861, 1871, 1881, 1891, 1901, 1911, 1921, 1931, and 1951.

COUNTIES at each CENSUS since 1755

BOTH SEXES				
1821	1831	1841	1851	1861
2,091,521	2,364,386	2,620,184	2,888,742	3,062,294
155,049	177,657	192,387	212,032	221,569
113,355	139,606	170,453	191,264	204,425
97,316	100,973	97,371	89,298	79,724
127,299	145,055	164,356	189,858	198,971
43,663	48,337	49,679	54,171	59,215
33,385	34,048	34,438	36,297	36,613
13,797	14,151	15,740	16,608	16,331
29,181	34,529	36,343	38,709	41,111
13,263	14,729	19,155	22,951	21,450
70,878	73,770	72,830	78,123	75,878
27,317	33,211	44,296	45,103	52,034
35,127	36,145	35,886	36,386	37,634
114,556	128,839	140,140	153,546	154,770
89,961	94,797	97,799	96,500	88,888
29,118	31,431	33,075	34,598	34,466
7,762	9,072	8,763	8,924	7,977
38,903	40,590	41,119	43,121	42,495
244,387	316,819	426,972	530,169	631,566
191,514	219,345	225,454	259,435	273,997
31,398	34,498	35,012	38,959	42,695
9,268	9,354	9,217	9,956	10,065
26,979	28,847	30,507	31,455	32,395
10,046	10,578	10,499	10,738	11,408
138,247	142,166	137,457	138,660	133,500
112,175	133,443	155,072	161,091	177,561
68,762	74,820	78,685	82,707	81,406
40,892	43,663	46,025	51,642	54,119
6,637	6,833	7,990	9,809	10,449
65,376	72,621	82,057	86,237	91,926
23,840	25,518	24,782	25,793	25,246
22,685	23,291	26,872	30,135	38,645
33,240	36,258	39,195	43,389	42,095
26,145	29,392	30,558	31,078	31,670

Military and Persons on board the Shipping in Scottish Harbours and

POPULATION of SCOTLAND and of the

COUNTIES	BOTH SEXES		
	1871	1881	1891
SCOTLAND . . .	3,360,018	3,735,573	4,025,647
1. Aberdeen . . .	244,603	267,990	281,332
2. Angus . . .	237,567	266,360	277,788
3. Argyll . . .	75,679	76,468	75,003
4. Ayr	200,809	217,519	226,283
5. Banff . . .	62,023	62,736	64,190
6. Berwick . . .	36,486	35,392	32,406
7. Bute . . .	16,977	17,657	18,404
8. Caithness . . .	39,992	38,865	37,177
9. Clackmannan . .	23,747	25,680	28,432
10. Dumfries . . .	74,808	76,140	74,221
11. Dunbarton . .	58,857	75,333	94,495
12. East Lothian . .	37,771	38,502	37,485
13. Fife	160,735	171,931	187,346
14. Inverness . . .	87,531	90,454	89,317
15. Kincardine . .	34,630	34,464	35,647
16. Kinross . . .	7,198	6,697	6,280
17. Kirkcudbright . .	41,859	42,127	39,985
18. Lanark . . .	765 339	904,412	1,046,040
19. Midlothian . .	328,379	389,164	434,159
20. Moray . . .	43,612	43,788	43,453
21. Nairn . . .	10,225	10,455	10,019
22. Orkney . . .	31,274	32,044	30,453
23. Peebles . . .	12,330	13,822	14,761
24. Perth . . .	127,768	129,007	126,184
25. Renfrew . . .	216,947	263,374	290,798
26. Ross and Cromarty .	80,955	78,547	77,810
27. Roxburgh . . .	53,974	53,442	53,741
28. Selkirk . . .	14,005	25,564	27,353
29. Stirling . . .	98,218	112,443	125,608
30. Sutherland . .	24,317	23,370	21,896
31. West Lothian . .	40,965	43,510	52,808
32. Wigtown . . .	38,830	38,611	36,062
33. Zetland . . .	31,608	29,705	28,711

NOTE.—The above numbers include the Military in 1841, and both Waters in 1851, 1861, 1871, 1881, 1891, 1901, 1911, 1921, 1931, and 1951.

—*continued*

COUNTIES at each CENSUS since 1755

BOTH SEXES				
1901	1911	1921	1931	1951
4,472,103	4,760,904	4,882,497	4,842,980	5,095,969
304,439	312,177	301,016	300,436	308,055
284,082	281,417	271,052	270,190	274,870
73,642	70,902	76,862	63,050	63,270
254,468	268,337	299,273	285,217	321,184
61,488	61,402	57,298	54,907	50,135
30,824	29,643	28,246	26,612	25,060
18,787	18,186	33,711	18,823	19,285
33,870	32,010	28,285	25,656	22,705
32,029	31,121	32,542	31,948	37,528
72,571	72,825	75,370	81,047	85,656
113,865	139,831	150,861	147,744	164,263
38,665	43,254	47,487	47,338	52,240
218,837	267,733	292,925	276,368	306,855
90,104	87,272	82,455	82,108	84,924
40,923	41,008	41,779	39,865	47,341
6,981	7,527	7,963	7,454	7,418
39,383	38,367	37,155	30,341	30,742
1,339,327	1,447,034	1,539,442	1,586,047	1,614,125
488,796	507,666	506,377	526,296	565,746
44,800	43,427	41,558	40,806	48,211
9,291	9,319	8,790	8,294	8,719
28,699	25,897	24,111	22,077	21,258
15,066	15,258	15,332	15,051	15,226
123,283	124,342	125,503	120,793	128,072
268,980	314,552	298,904	288,586	324,652
76,450	77,364	70,818	62,799	60,503
48,804	47,192	44,989	45,788	45,562
23,356	24,601	22,607	22,608	21,724
142,291	160,991	161,719	166,447	187,432
21,440	20,179	17,802	16,101	13,664
65,711	80,161	83,962	81,431	88,576
32,685	31,998	30,783	29,331	31,625
28,166	27,911	25,520	21,421	19,343

Military and Persons on board the Shipping in Scottish Harbours and

INTERCENSAL INCREASE or DECREASE of POPULATION

COUNTIES	BOTH SEXES		
	1755 to 1801	1801 to 1811	1811 to 1821
SCOTLAND . . .	343,040	197,444	285,657
1. Aberdeen . . .	4,897	12,806	21,178
2. Angus . . .	30,170	8,134	6,168
3. Argyll . . .	14,991	5,264	10,775
4. Ayr	25,198	19,632	23,460
5. Banff . . .	−1,262	1,217	5,230
6. Berwick . . .	6,219	687	2,492
7. Bute . . .	4,666	242	1,764
8. Caithness . . .	394	810	5,762
9. Clackmannan . .	1,855	1,152	1,253
10. Dumfries . . .	14,809	8,363	7,918
11. Dunbarton . .	6,853	3,479	3,128
12. East Lothian . .	277	1,064	4,077
13. Fife	12,173	7,529	13,284
14. Inverness . . .	13,109	4,999	12,290
15. Kincardine . .	3,292	1,090	1,679
16. Kinross . . .	1,836	520	517
17. Kirkcudbright . .	8,006	4,473	5,219
18. Lanark . . .	65,966	43,599	53,096
19. Midlothian . .	32,185	26,010	42,907
20. Moray . . .	−2,844	207	3,431
21. Nairn . . .	2,628	174	772
22. Orkney . . .	1,064	−1,207	3,741
23. Peebles . . .	−173	1,200	111
24. Perth . . .	5,467	8,807	3,857
25. Renfrew . . .	51,856	14,671	19,003
26. Ross and Cromarty .	8,234	4,535	7,909
27. Roxburgh . . .	−983	3,509	3,662
28. Selkirk . . .	1,367	501	748
29. Stirling . . .	13,811	7,349	7,202
30. Sutherland . .	2,343	512	211
31. West Lothian . .	1,015	1,607	3,234
32. Wigtown . . .	6,452	3,973	6,349
33. Zetland . . .	7,169	536	3,230

of SCOTLAND and of the COUNTIES since 1755

BOTH SEXES				
1821 to 1831	1831 to 1841	1841 to 1851	1851 to 1861	1861 to 1871
272,865	255,798	268,558	173,552	297,724
22,608	14,730	19,645	9,537	23,034
26,251	30,847	20,811	13,161	33,142
3,657	−3,602	−8,073	−9,574	−4,045
17,756	19,301	25,502	9,113	1,838
4,674	1,342	4,492	5,044	2,808
663	390	1,859	316	−127
354	1,589	868	−277	646
5,348	1,814	2,366	2,402	−1,119
1,466	4,426	3,796	−1,501	2,297
2,892	−940	5,293	−2,245	−1,070
5,894	11,085	807	6,931	6,823
1,018	−259	500	1,248	137
14,283	11,301	13,406	1,224	5,965
4,836	3,002	−1,299	−7,612	−1,357
2,313	1,644	1,523	−132	164
1,310	−309	161	−947	−779
1,687	529	2,002	−626	−636
72,432	110,153	103,197	101,397	133,773
27,831	6,109	33,981	14,562	54,382
3,100	514	3,947	3,736	917
86	−137	739	109	160
1,868	1,660	948	940	−1,121
532	−79	239	670	922
3,919	−4,709	1,203	−5,160	−5,732
21,268	21,629	6,019	16,470	39,386
6,058	3,865	4,022	−1,301	−451
2,771	2,362	5,617	2,477	−145
196	1,157	1,819	640	3,556
7,245	9,436	4,180	5,689	6,292
1,678	−736	1,011	−547	−929
606	3,581	3,263	8,510	2,320
3,018	2,937	4,194	−1,294	−3,265
3,247	1,166	520	592	−62

INTERCENSAL INCREASE or DECREASE of POPULATION

COUNTIES	BOTH SEXES	
	1871 to 1881	1881 to 1891
SCOTLAND	375,555	290,074
1. Aberdeen	23,387	13,342
2. Angus	28,793	11,428
3. Argyll	789	−1,465
4. Ayr	16,710	8,764
5. Banff	713	1,454
6. Berwick	−1,094	−2,986
7. Bute	680	747
8. Caithness	−1,127	−1,688
9. Clackmannan	1,933	2,752
10. Dumfries	1,332	−1,919
11. Dunbarton	16,476	19,162
12. East Lothian	731	−1,017
13. Fife	11,196	15,415
14. Inverness	2,923	−1,137
15. Kincardine	−166	1,183
16. Kinross	−501	−417
17. Kirkcudbright	268	−2,142
18. Lanark	139,073	141,628
19. Midlothian	60,785	44,995
20. Moray	176	−335
21. Nairn	230	−436
22. Orkney	770	−1,591
23. Peebles	1,492	939
24. Perth	1,239	−2,823
25. Renfrew	46,427	27,424
26. Ross and Cromarty . . .	−2,408	−737
27. Roxburgh	−532	299
28. Selkirk	11,559	1,789
29. Stirling	14,225	13,165
30. Sutherland	−947	−1,474
31. West Lothian	2,545	9,298
32. Wigtown	−219	−2,549
33. Zetland	−1,903	−994

—continued

of SCOTLAND and of the COUNTIES since 1755

BOTH SEXES				
1891 to 1901	1901 to 1911	1911 to 1921	1921 to 1931	1931 to 1951
446,456	288,801	121,593	−39,517	252,989
23,107	7,738	−11,161	−580	7,619
6,294	−2,665	−10,365	−862	4,680
−1,361	−2,740	5,960	−13,812	220
28,185	13,869	30,936	−14,056	35,967
−2,702	−86	−4,104	−2,391	−4,772
−1,582	−1,181	−1,397	−1,634	−1,552
383	−601	15,525	−14,888	462
−3,307	−1,860	−3,725	−2,629	−2,951
3,597	−908	1,421	−594	5,580
−1,650	254	2,545	5,677	4,609
19,370	25,966	11,030	−3,117	16,519
1,180	4,589	4,233	−149	4,902
31,491	48,896	25,192	−16,557	30,487
787	−2,832	−4,817	−347	2,816
5,276	85	771	−1,914	7,476
701	546	436	−509	−36
−602	−1,016	−1,212	−6,814	401
293,287	107,707	92,408	46,605	28,078
54,637	18,870	−1,289	19,919	39,450
1,347	−1,373	−1,869	−752	7,405
−728	28	−529	−496	425
−1,754	−2,802	−1,786	−2,034	−819
305	192	74	−281	175
−2,901	1,059	1,161	−4,710	7,279
−21,818	45,572	−15,648	−10,318	36,066
−1,360	914	−6,546	−8,019	−2,296
−4,937	−1,612	−2,203	799	−226
−3,997	1,245	−1,994	1	−884
16,683	18,700	728	4,728	20,985
−456	−1,261	−2,377	−1,701	−2,437
12,903	14,450	3,801	−2,531	7,145
−3,377	−687	−1,215	−1,452	2,294
−545	−255	−2,391	−4,099	−2,078

POLL TAX RETURNS

These list the names of residences and the names of everyone over 16 years of age, including women. So far as is known the following is a complete list of those now extant.

Parish of Abercorn		1694
Straithbrock		
Ecclesmachen		
Shire of Aberdeen		1696
Burgh of Anstruther Wester		1694
Shire of Banff	c.	1694
Shire of Berwickshire		1695
Parish of Bathgate		1694
Bo'ness and Kinneil		
Carriden		1995
Dalmeny		1694
Edinburgh and Leith		
Parish of Houston		1695
Inchinnan	c.	1694
Kilbarchan		1695
Kilellan		
Kilmalcolm		1694
Lesmahagow (& Lanark)		
Livingstoun		
Torphichen		
Shire of Orkney		
Renfrew		
Argyll		
Perth		
Burgh of St. Andrews		

HEARTH TAX ROLLS

These give lists of hearths, with names of householders. All are included as those who paid, did not pay, and the poor, were all listed. The extant lists are almost complete for Scotland. Only the northernmost counties are omitted, though Sutherland is included. The date is 1683-84.

SEAFORTH PAPERS

1797

These include a circular letter from Henry Dundas, Home Secretary, to the Lord-Lieutenant of Ross (Seaforth) containing proposals relating to the formation of a Volunteer Corps, mentioning *inter alia* a census of persons between 15 and 60. This census for Ross is included in the papers. It is done by parishes with totals. There is also a particular census of men between 19 and 23. (Included in this collection is a list of persons in the parish of Ness, which gives the names of heads of families with number of persons in the family, with totals of families and numbers of persons in " Townships ").

The military census extant for Ross must have been carried out for other counties, but the present whereabouts of the records is unknown.

INDEX

Kilbride, Arran, parish of, 32.
——, Ayrshire. *See* Kilbride, West.
——, Lanarkshire. *See* Kilbride, East.
——, East, parish of, 30.
——, West, parish of, 27.
Kilbucho, parish of, 17.
Kilcalmonell, parish of, 33 and *n*.
Kilchoman, parish of, 33.
Kilchrenan, parish of, 33.
Kilconquhar, parish of, 40.
Kildalton, parish of, 33.
Kildonan, parish of, xxviii, 63.
Kildrummy, parish of, 53.
Kilellan. *See* Killellan.
Kilernan. *See* Killearnan.
Kilfinan, parish of, 33.
Kilfinichen (Kilfinchen), parish of, 34.
Killallan. *See* Killellan.
Killarrow (Killarow), parish of, 33.
Killean, parish of, 34.
Killearn, parish of, 37.
Killearnan (Kilernan), parish of, 61.
Killellan (Kilellan, Killallan), parish of, 31 and *n*, 90.
Killin, parish of, 44.
Kilmadock, parish of, 44.
Kilmalcolm, parish of, 31, 90.
Kilmallie (Kilmalie), parish of, 60 and *n*.
Kilmanivaig. *See* Kilmonivaig.
Kilmany, parish of, 40.
Kilmarnock, parish of, 27.
Kilmaronock, parish of, 35.
Kilmartin (Kilmartine), parish of, 34.
Kilmaurs, parish of, 27.
Kilmichael-Glassary (Kilmichael), parish of, 34.
Kilmodan, parish of, 34.
Kilmonivaig (Kilmanivaig), parish of, 34.
Kilmorack (Kilmorak), parish of, 60.
Kilmore, parish of, 34.
Kilmory (Kilmorie), parish of, 32.
Kilmuir, parish of, 60.
——, Easter, parish of, 61 and *n*.
——, Wester, parish of, 61.
Kilninian, parish of, 34.
Kilninver, parish of, 34.
Kilpatrick, East, parish of, 35.
——, West, parish of, 35.
Kilrenny, parish of, 40.
Kilspindie, parish of, 44.
Kilsyth, parish of, 37.
Kiltarlity, parish of, 60.

Kiltearn, parish of, 61.
Kilwinning, parish of, 27.
Kincardin Oneil. *See* Kincardine O'Neil.
Kincardine (Kincardin), county of, xxxvii, 5, 49-50, 72-73, 82-85, 86-89.
——, Perthshire, parish of, 44.
——, Ross-shire, parish of, 61 and *n*.
—— O'Neil (Kincardin Oneil), parish of, 53.
Kinclaven (Kinclavin), parish of, 44.
Kinellar (Kinnellar), parish of, 53.
Kinfauns, parish of, 44.
King Edward, parish of, 53.
Kingarth, parish of, 32.
Kinghorn, parish of, 40.
Kinglassie, parish of, 40.
Kingoldrum, parish of, 48.
Kingsbarns, parish of, 40.
Kingussie (Kinguissie), parish of, 60.
Kinkell, parish of, 53 and *n*.
Kinloch, parish of, 44.
Kinloss, parish of, 58.
Kinnaird, Angus, parish of, 47 and *n*.
——, Perthshire, parish of, 44.
Kinneff, parish of, 50.
Kinneil, parish of, 90.
Kinnell (Kinnel), parish of, 47.
Kinnellar. *See* Kinellar.
Kinnethmont. *See* Kennethmont.
Kinnettles, parish of, 48.
Kinnoull (Kinnoul), parish of, 44.
Kinross, county of, xxxvii, 5, 38, 72-73, 82-85, 86-89.
——, parish of, 38.
Kintail, parish of, xxviii, 61.
Kintore, parish of, 53.
Kintyre, district of, 70.
——, Mull of, 70.
Kippen, parish of, 44.
Kirk of Dollar. *See* Dollar.
Kirk of Dores. *See* Durris, Kirkton of.
Kirkbean, parish of, 24.
Kirkcaldy (Kirkaldy), parish of, 40.
Kirkcolm, parish of, 25.
Kirkconnel, parish of, 22.
Kirkcowan, parish of, 25.
Kirkcudbright, county of, 5, 23-24, 68-69, 82-85, 86-89.
——, parish of, 24.
——, town of, 68.
Kirkden, parish of, 47.
Kirkgunzeon, parish of, 24.
Kirkhill, parish of, 60.

Lochlaxford. *See* Laxford, Loch.
Lochlee, parish of, 48.
Lochmaben, parish of, 22.
Lochmonnar. *See* Monar, Loch.
Lochrutton, parish of, 24.
Lochs, parish of, 62.
Lochshelly. *See* Seilge, Loch na.
Lochshinn. *See* Shin, Loch.
Lochtreag. *See* Treig, Loch.
Lochwinnoch, parish of, 32.
Logie, Angus, parish of, 48.
——, Fife, parish of, 41.
——, Stirlingshire, parish of, 44.
—— -Buchan, parish of, 53.
—— -Coldstone (Logie Colstone), parish of, 53.
—— -Easter, parish of, 62 and *n.*
Logierait, parish of, 44.
Lomond, Loch, 70.
London, city of, xiv, xvi, 79 and *n.*
Long, Loch, 71.
Longbride. *See* Lhanbryd.
Longforgan, parish of, 44.
Longformacus, parish of, 12.
Longmay. *See* Lonmay.
Longside, parish of, 54.
Lonmay (Longmay), parish of, 53.
Lorn, district of, 70.
Loth, parish of, 63.
Loudoun, parish of, 27.
Lowes (Lows), Loch of the, Selkirk-shire, 68.
Luce, New, parish of, 25.
Lumphanan, parish of, 54.
Lunan, parish of, 48.
Lundie and Fowlis, parish of, 48 and *n.*
Luss, parish of, 35.
Lyne, parish of, 17.

Machar, New, parish of, 54.
——, Old, parish of, 51*n*, 54.
Mackerston. *See* Makerstoun.
Madderty (Maderty), parish of, 45.
Mains, parish of, 48.
Makerstoun (Mackerston), parish of, 20.
Manor (Manner), parish of, 18.
Mar (Marr), district of, 72.
March. *See* Merse.
Markinch, parish of, 41.
Marnoch (Marnock), parish of, 57.
Marr. *See* Mar.
Maryculter, parish of, 50.
Marykirk, parish of, 50.
Maryton, parish of, 48.
Mauchline, parish of, 27.
Maxton, parish of, 20.

Maybole, parish of, 27.
Mearns, The, district of, 72.
——, parish of, 32.
Meigle, parish of, 45.
Meldrum, Old, parish of, 54.
Melrose, parish of, 20.
——, town of, 68.
Melville, Henry Dundas, 1st vis-count, corresponds with Lord-Lieutenant of Ross about the formation of a Volunteer Corps, 91.
Menach Water. *See* Minnoch Water.
Menmuir, parish of, 48.
Menteith (Monteith), district of, 72.
Merse (March), district of, 68.
Mertoun (Merton), parish of, 12.
Methlick, parish of, 54.
Methven, parish of, 45.
Mid Calder. *See* Calder, Mid.
Middlebie, parish of, 22.
Midlothian, county of, xviii, xxv-xxvi, xxxv, 5, 14-16, 68-69, 82-85, 86-89.
Midmar, parish of, 54.
Minnigaff, parish of, 24.
——, village of, 69.
Minnoch (Menach) Water, 70.
Minto, parish of, 20.
Mochrum, parish of, 25.
Moffat, parish of, 22.
Moidart, district of, 33*n*, 74.
Monar, Loch (Lochmonnar), 74.
Moneydie (Monedie), parish of, 45.
Monifieth, parish of, 48.
Monikie, parish of, 48.
Monimail (Monymail), parish of, 41.
Monivaird. *See* Monzievaird.
Monkland, East, parish of, 30.
——, West, parish of, 30.
Monkton, parish of, 27.
Monquhitter (Monwhitter), parish of, 54.
Monteith. *See* Menteith.
Montrose, parish of, 48.
Monwhitter. *See* Monquhitter.
Monymail. *See* Monimail.
Monymusk, parish of, 54.
Monzie, parish of, 45.
Monzievaird (Monivaird), parish of, 45.
Moonzie, parish of, 41.
Morar, district of, 33*n.*
Moray, county of, xxxvii, 5, 57-58, 74-75, 82-85, 86-89.
Morbattle. *See* Morebattle.
Mordington, parish of, 12.

K *

REPORT OF THE SIXTY-THIRD
ANNUAL MEETING OF THE
SCOTTISH HISTORY SOCIETY

THE SIXTY-THIRD ANNUAL MEETING OF THE SOCIETY was
held in the Rooms of the Royal Society, George Street,
Edinburgh, on Saturday, 17th December 1949, at 3 P.M.

The Rt. Hon. Lord Cooper, LL.D., President of the
Society, was in the Chair.

The Report of the Council was as follows :—

It is with deep regret that the Council have to record
the death of one of the Society's oldest and most valued
members—Dr. W. K. Dickson. Dr. Dickson joined the
Society in 1890 and was elected in 1908 to the Council,
of which he remained a member till his death, being Chairman from 1934 to 1938. He edited one of the Society's
volumes for 1894-95—*The Jacobite Attempt of 1719*—
and forty years later another volume—*Correspondence of
Sir George Warrender*. For the *Miscellany Volume VI* he
edited *Memories of Ayrshire about 1780 by the Reverend
John Mitchell, D.D.*, and at the time of the Society's jubilee
in 1936 he compiled a short history of its activities which
is bound up with *Volume XXIX* of the *Third Series*. By

his scholarship, his geniality and his ready wit he endeared himself to his colleagues on the Council as to all his friends.

The Council are much concerned at the slowness with which the Society's volumes pass through the press. At the time of last year's report the *Accounts of the Collectors of the Thirds of Benefices*, edited by Dr. Gordon Donaldson, was already in proof apart from the index. It is now being bound and should be issued to members shortly.

Miscellany Volume VIII, to be issued for the year 1948-49, has (except one item) been with the printer for some months and it is hoped that proofs may soon be forthcoming. It will include *Early Monastic Charters*, edited by Dr. D. E. Easson ; *Letter of James III to the Duke of Burgundy*, edited by Mr. John Armstrong ; *The English Army at Flodden*, edited by Professor J. D. Mackie ; *Letter from Lord Chancellor Glamis to Theodore Beza*, edited by Dr. Gordon Donaldson ; *Documents Relating to the Grandson of Prince Charles Edward*, edited by Miss Henrietta Tayler ; and *Papers of a Renfrewshire Farm*, edited by Dr. G. S. Pryde.

For 1949-50 the Council propose to issue a volume of *Scottish Population Statistics*, edited by Mr. J. G. Kyd, for 1950-51 *Kirkintilloch Burgh Court Book, 1658-1694*, edited by Dr. G. S. Pryde, and for 1951-52 *Letters of James IV*, edited by Mr. R. L. Mackie. For a later volume they are considering the issue of *Report (and Continuation) of the Proceedings of the Convention of Estates in Scotland*—a periodical printed in London from March 1689 to October 1690, and consisting altogether of 147 numbers. While some separate numbers are contained in various libraries, only one seems to possess a complete set bound together.

Professor J. D. Mackie, having completed the normal period of four years, has retired from the chairmanship of the Council and has been succeeded by Professor W. Croft Dickinson. The Council desire to express their appreciation of the services of Professor Mackie in that capacity.

Members of Council who retire in rotation at this time are Dr. H. W. Meikle, Dr. Annie I. Dunlop and Mr. H. M. Paton. Dr. Angus has also expressed a wish to retire. The Council feel that they cannot allow Dr. Angus' resignation to take effect without placing on record their sense of the valuable help he has given to the Society as Assistant Secretary from 1920 to 1924, as Joint Secretary from 1924 to 1928 and again as a member of Council since 1940. His unique knowledge of Scottish archives has always been placed unreservedly at the service of the Society and of all workers in the field of Scottish history. The Council recommend the re-election of Dr. Meikle, Dr. Dunlop and Mr. Paton, and the election of Professor Mackie in place of Professor Dickinson. They also recommend the election of Miss Henrietta Tayler and Mr. James Fergusson in place of Dr. Angus and the late Dr. Dickson.

The Society has lost during the year 13 members by death or resignation ; the names of 4 others, whose subscriptions were in arrear, have been removed from the list ; 13 new members have joined. The total membership, including 145 libraries, is now 407.

An Abstract of the Accounts for 1948-49, as audited, is appended.

Professor W. Croft Dickinson, Chairman of the Council, in moving the adoption of the Report and Accounts, paid tribute to the work of his predecessor, Professor Mackie, and also to the late Dr. W. K. Dickson and to Dr. W. Angus. He pointed out that from the apparent balance of £408 the volume for the past year fell to be paid and appealed for more members and more covenanted subscriptions if the work of the Society for Scottish history was to be maintained.

Dr. Douglas Guthrie seconded, and the Report and Accounts were unanimously approved.

The President then delivered an address entitled ' The Declaration of Arbroath Revisited.' He argued from an analysis of the prose rhythms and other peculiarities that the Declaration and five other state papers of the period had all been drafted by the Abbot Bernard de Linton, and showed from papal records that the original Declaration and a private letter from Bruce were delivered to the Pope at Avignon by early July 1320. The document preserved in the Register House could only be a duplicate.

Referring to the teaching of Scottish History, Lord Cooper said that Scotland must be the only advanced country in the world which did nothing to ensure that its youth were taught the story of their nation's past. The Leaving Certificates put a premium on English, Greek, Roman, European and Colonial History ; but unless a candidate wished to try one of the optional questions on Scotland, which very few did, Scottish History could safely be ignored altogether. At any Scottish University it was possible to graduate with first-class honours in History without professing acquaintance with the history of Scotland. At Edinburgh University Scottish History was one of eleven options, another being the History of East Africa ! There was a subject called British History which proved on examination to be English History with occasional side glances at Scotland through English spectacles at times when Scotland crossed England's path. The history schools of every other country put the history of their own country first.

Whatever its true purpose, Scotland's educational policy was certainly well calculated to condition the youthful Scottish mind into gazing instinctively towards London with something of the submissive awe with which devout Moslems turned towards Mecca.

A vote of thanks to Lord Cooper for his address and for his services to the Society during the term of his presidency was moved by Professor J. D. Mackie, who referred to him as a patron, defender and genuine student of the history of our country.

The President then entertained the Society to tea.

ABSTRACT Account of Charge and Discharge of the Intromissions of the Honorary Treasurer for the year from 1st November 1948 to 31st October 1949.

CHARGE.

I. Cash in Bank at close of Account for year ended 1st November 1948—

    1. Sum at credit of Savings Account with Bank of Scotland . . £135 0 7

    2. Sum at credit of Current Account with Bank of Scotland . . 52 10 0

    3. Cash in hands of Bank of Scotland to meet current postages . 0 7 0½

                             £187 17 7½

II. Subscriptions received 406 8 0

III. Past publications sold (including postages recovered from purchasers) . . . 11 6 6

IV. Interest on Savings Account with Bank of Scotland 2 0 6

V. Refund of Income Tax 57 11 0

VI. Miscellaneous 0 8 1

VII. Sums drawn from Bank Current Account. . £256 19 9

VIII. Sums drawn from Bank Savings Account. . —

                             £665 11 8½

DISCHARGE.

I. Cost of printing Publications
during year . . £206 0 0
Cost of printing Annual Report
and Printers' postages, etc. 16 11 8
——————— £222 11 8

II. Miscellaneous payments, including Bank's
postages 34 14 0½

III. Sums lodged in Bank Current
Account . . . £475 13 7

IV. Sums lodged in Bank Savings
Account . . . £2 0 6

V. Funds at close of this Account—

   1. Balance at credit of
Savings Account with
Bank of Scotland . £137 1 1

   2. Balance at credit of
Current Account with
Bank of Scotland . 271 3 10

   3. Cash in hands of Bank of
Scotland to meet cur-
rent postages . 0 1 1
——————— 408 6 0

£665 11 8½

EDINBURGH, 9th *November* 1949.—I have examined the Accounts of
the Honorary Treasurer of the Scottish History Society for the year from
1st November 1948 to 31st October 1949, and I find the same to be
correctly stated and sufficiently vouched.

HENRY M. PATON,
Auditor.

Scottish History Society

LIST OF MEMBERS

1st November 1949

LIST OF MEMBERS

Her Majesty Queen Mary.

Adam, Lt.-Commander Charles Keith, R.N., Blair-Adam, Kinross-shire.

Adamson, Miss Margot Robert, 100 Handside Lane, Welwyn Garden City, Herts.

Agnew, Rev. A. T., M.A., B.D., H.C.F., St. George's Vicarage, Shrewsbury.

Alexander, Joseph, 108 Glengate, Kirriemuir.

Allan, Mrs. Jessie S., 122 Dorrator Road, Camelon, Falkirk.

Allan, John, M.R.C.V.S., Castle-Douglas.

Angus, William, LL.D., 69 Cluny Gardens, Edinburgh.

Armet, Miss Catherine M., 42 Main Street, Davidson's Mains, Edinburgh.

10 Baird, Mrs. J. G. A., 9 Learmonth Terrace, Edinburgh.

Balfour-Melville, E. W. M., D.Litt., 2 South Learmonth Gardens, Edinburgh (*Hon. Secretary*).

Barron, Evan M., *Inverness Courier*, Inverness.

Baxter, Professor J. H., D.D., D.Litt., 71 South Street, St. Andrews.

Bayne, Mrs. Neil, 51 Ann Street, Edinburgh.

Begg, F. J. Henderson, M.B., Ch.B., Strathbeg, Barton Court Avenue, New Milton, Hants.

Birrell, Mrs. N. Dow, 10 Canmore Street, Dunfermline.

Boase, Edward R., Advocate, Westoun, Wardlaw Gardens, St. Andrews.

Bonar, John James, Eldinbrae, Lasswade.

Boyd, Edward, C.A., 27 Melville Street, Edinburgh.

20 Boyd, Mrs. Helen T., 22 Belgrave Crescent, Edinburgh.

Browning, Professor Andrew, M.A., Westdel, Queen's Place, Glasgow, W. 2.

Buchan, J. Walter, Bank House, Peebles.

Buchanan, G. A., Gask House, Auchterarder.

Buchanan, Hugh, Private Bag, Taihape, New Zealand.

Buchanan, H. R., 172 St. Vincent Street, Glasgow.

Buchanan, John, 67 Great King Street, Edinburgh.

Buist, Frank D. J., The Hollies, Broughty Ferry, Angus.

Bulloch, Rev. James, Manse of Tranent, East Lothian.

Bute, The Marquess of, Mountstuart, Isle of Bute.

30 Buyers, John A., Poundland House, Pinwherry, by Girvan, Ayrshire.

CAMERON, Lt.-Colonel ANGUS, Firhall, Nairn.

Cameron-Swan, Captain Donald, F.R.A.S., F.S.A.Scot., The Gables, Ravensberg Avenue, Newlands, Cape Town.

Campbell, Buchanan, W.S., Moidart, Currie, Midlothian.

Campbell, Douglas, 44 Wall Street, New York, U.S.A.

Campbell, Sir George I., of Succoth, Bart., Crarae, Minard, Argyll.

Campbell, J. L., of Canna, Isle of Canna.

Campbell, Mrs. Margaret M., LL.B., 8 Kirklee Quadrant, Glasgow.

Campbell, Rev. William M., The Manse, Barloan, Dumbarton.

Cant, Rev. Alan, 2 Kinburn Place, St. Andrews.

40 Carmichael, Evelyn G. M., of Carmichael, O.B.E., Berrington Hall, Shrewsbury.

Carmichael, J. L., Arthurstone, Meigle, Perthshire.

Clark, Mrs. James, Ravelston, Blackhall, Midlothian.

Cleary, Vincent, Bank of Montreal, Canada.

Colquhoun, Rev. John, Free Presbyterian Manse, Glendale, Isle of Skye.

Conway, G. R. G., M.Inst.C.E., Apartado, 124 Bis, Mexico, D. F., Mexico.

Cooper, The Right Hon. Lord, LL.D., 16 Hermitage Drive, Edinburgh.

Corsar, Kenneth Charles, F.S.A.Scot., Mauricewood, Milton Bridge, Midlothian.

Cowan, Miss Lillias A., Arden Hotel, 19 Royal Terrace, Edinburgh.

Cowie, John, 20 Blythswood Square, Glasgow, C. 2.

50 Crichton-Stuart, The Lord Colum, Ardencraig, Rothesay, Bute.

Cross, A. R., B.A., Old Ballikinrain, Balfron, Stirlingshire.

Cunningham, Miss A., 15 Murrayfield Gardens, Edinburgh.

DALGLEISH, Rev. G. W., M.A., The Manse, Monymusk, Aberdeenshire.

Dalyell, of the Binns, Lt.-Colonel Gordon, C.I.E., D.L., Linlithgow.

Darling, James Stormonth, W.S., Edenbank, Kelso.

Davidson, Captain Duncan G., of Flemington, Gollanfield, Inverness-shire.

Davidson, W. L., C.A., 142 St. Vincent Street, Glasgow, C. 2.

Davies, Professor Godfrey, 395 South Bonnie Avenue, Pasadena, California, U.S.A.

De Beer, E. S., M.A., 11 Sussex Place, Regent's Park, London, N.W. 1.

60 Dickinson, Miss G., Westfield College, Hampstead, London, N.W. 3.

Dickinson, Professor W. C., Ph.D., D.Lit., 18 Frogstone Road West, Edinburgh.

Dickson, A. Hope, 9 Succoth Gardens, Edinburgh.

Dickson, C. H., 8 Highwood Gardens, Ilford, Essex.

Dickson, J. Douglas H., Mus. Doc., W.S., 7 Doune Terrace, Edinburgh (*Hon. Treasurer*).

Dickson, Walter, Lynedoch House, Elcho Terrace, Portobello.

Dickson, Walter S., Advocate, 6 Circus Gardens, Edinburgh.

Dobie, M. R., National Library of Scotland, Edinburgh.

Don, Captain William G., Maulesden, Brechin, Angus.

Donaldson, Gordon, Ph.D., 24 East Hermitage Place, Edinburgh.

70 Donnelly, H. H., LL.B., Scottish Education Department, St. Andrew's House, Edinburgh.

Duncan, Archd. A. M., Queen's University, Belfast.

Dunlop, Mrs. Annie I., O.B.E., Ph.D., D.Litt., Dunselma, Fenwick, Ayrshire.

Dunlop, G. B., *Standard* Office, 3 Duke Street, Kilmarnock.

Dunlop, George, Craigrossie, 5 Divert Road, Gourock.

Easson, Rev. D. E., B.D., Ph.D., 48 Delph Lane, Leeds, 6.

Elliot, Miss Effie M., Balnakiel House, Durness, Sutherland.

Elrick, W. J. H., c/o Bank of New South Wales, 29 Thread-needle Street, London, E.C. 2.

Fairgrieve, Andrew, Maplehurst, Galashiels.

Fergusson, James, Kilkerran, Maybole, Ayrshire.

80 Finlayson, Rev. Angus, Free Church Manse, North Tolsta, Stornoway.

Fleming, A. Gibb, Woodlands House, Milngavie, Dumbartonshire.

Fletcher, Sir Angus S., K.C.M.G., C.B.E., East Hampton, New York, U.S.A.

Flood, Captain William A. S., O.B.E., M.C., St. Louis, Banbury, Oxon.

Forbes, Sir G. Ogilvie, K.C.M.G., D.L., of Boyndlie, Fraserburgh.

Fordyce, Professor C. J., The University, Glasgow.

Forrest, Colonel J. V., C.B., C.M.G., Glenmachan, Strandtown, Belfast.

Forrester, Rev. D. M., B.D., U.F. Manse, Broughton, Peeblesshire.

Foulis, George H. Liston, 6 Drumsheugh Place, Edinburgh.

Fraser, Charles Ian, of Reelig, Kirkhill, Inverness-shire.

90 Franklin, Thomas Bedford, M.A., F.R.S.E., 16 Learmonth Place, Edinburgh.

Galbraith, Professor V. H., F.B.A., Oriel College, Oxford.

Galloway, T. L., of Auchendrane, by Ayr.

Gauld, H. Drummond, Craighead, Whitehills, Banffshire.

Gent, Frank, O.B.E., 20 Great Stuart Street, Edinburgh.

Gibb, Sir Alexander, C.B.E., C.B., LL.D., F.R.S., Queen Anne's Lodge, Westminster, London, S.W. 1.

Gillies, Rev. W. A., D.D., 96 Bonnyrigg Road, Eskbank, Dalkeith.

Grant, Sir Francis J., K.C.V.O., LL.D., W.S., 18 George Square, Edinburgh.

Grant, Sir Francis, Bart., House of Monymusk, Monymusk, Aberdeenshire.

Gray, Col. W. B., C.B.E., c/o Lloyds Bank Ltd., Cox's & King's Branch, London, S.W. 1.

100 Grierson, Henry J., W.S., Laguna, Murthly, Perthshire.

Guthrie, Charles, W.S., 9 Great Stuart Street, Edinburgh.

Guthrie, Douglas, M.D., F.R.C.S., 21 Clarendon Crescent, Edinburgh.

HAY, Lt.-General Sir ROBERT, 44 Blacket Place, Edinburgh.

Hay, W. J., John Knox's House, Edinburgh.

Hayward, Robert S., The Hawthorns, Galashiels.

Henderson, Miss E. B., Nether Parkley, Linlithgow.

Henderson, Prof. Robert Candlish, K.C., 6 Doune Terrace, Edinburgh.

Hesketh, Lady, Powcester, Northamptonshire.

Hope, Major Archibald John George, of Luffness, Aberlady.

110 Hope, Miss Constance L., 19 Fenton Street, Alloa.

Hornel, Miss E. H., Broughton House, Kirkcudbright.

Horridge, Captain W., M.C., F.C.S., F.R.S.A., Heather Lea, Bury.

Hunter, J. N. W., Ph.D., Moray House Training College, Holyrood Road, Edinburgh.

Hutchison, David M., 170 Hope Street, Glasgow.

INNES, Sir THOMAS, of Learney, K.C.V.O., Lord Lyon King of Arms, H.M. General Register House, Edinburgh.

Insh, G. P., C.B.E., D.Litt., Ardenvohr, Bothwell, Lanarkshire.

Inverchapel, The Lord, Inverchapel, Loch Eck, by Dunoon, Argyllshire.

JAMIESON, The Right Hon. Lord, 34 Moray Place, Edinburgh.

Jarvis, R. C., ' Shelley,' Station Road, Hockley, near Southend, Essex.

120 Johnson, Norman Miller, B.Sc., F.R.S.E., &c., The Hainin, Gauldry, by Dundee.

Johnston, The Right Hon. Thomas, Monteviot, Kirkintilloch.

Johnston, Miss M. B., 18 Montpelier Terrace, Edinburgh.

KAY, ALEX., of M'Clure, Naismith, Brodie & Co., Glasgow.

Keir, Sir David Lindsay, The Master's Lodgings, Balliol College, Oxford.

Kilpatrick, P. J. W., Bridgend, Colinton.

King, Cecil H., Cushine House, Alford, Aberdeenshire.

Knox, J. M., 57 St. Vincent Street, Glasgow.

LAING, JOHN E., 20 Bridge Street, Glasgow, C. 5.

Leiper, R. J., Tomphubil, Foss, by Pitlochry.

130 Lightbody, John, Solicitor, 8 St. Colme Street, Edinburgh.

Lindsay, Rev. and Hon. E. R., The Presbytery, Stone, Staffs.

Loch, Laurence John Carysfort, 1st Kumaon Rifles, c/o Lloyds Bank Ltd., Hornby Road, Bombay.

Loch, Sydney, American Farm School, Thessaloniki, Greece.

Lochhead, Miss Marion, The Beeches, Wishaw, Lanarkshire.

Longmuir, Rev. J. Boyd, M.A., B.L., Manse of Swinton, Duns, Berwickshire.

Lorimer, W. L., 19 Murray Park, St. Andrews, Fife.

MACARTHUR, NEIL, Solicitor, Royal Bank Buildings, Inverness.

McAulay, Alex. C., 83 Sunnybank Street, Glasgow, S.E.

MacDonald, Sir Murdoch, K.C.M.G., 72 Victoria Street, London, S.W. 1.

140 Macfarlane-Grieve, Lt.-Colonel A. A., M.C., M.A., Woodslee, Canonbie, Dumfriesshire.

Macfarlane, George R., 1629 Harwood Street, Vancouver, B.C., Canada.

Macinnes, C. T., H.M. Register House, Edinburgh.

M'Intosh, Murdoch, Drummond Tower, Upper Drummond, Inverness.

Mackay, Æneas, 44 Craigs, Stirling.

Mackay, William, Netherwood, Inverness.

Mackechnie, Donald, Schoolhouse, Bridge of Douglas, Inveraray.

McKechnie, Hector, B.A., LL.B., K.C., 64 Great King Street, Edinburgh.

Mackechnie, Rev. John, M.A., B.D., F.S.A.Scot., 3 Eldon Terrace, Glasgow, W.

Mackenzie, Compton, Denchworth Manor, Wantage, Berks.

150 Mackenzie, Mrs. P. C., 7 Stainforth Road, Newbury Park, Essex.

Mackenzie, William C., Deargaill, St. Margarets-on-Thames.

M'Kerral, Andrew, C.I.E., M.A., B.Sc., Morton, Midcalder.

M'Kerrow, James A., Rickerby, Lochanhead, Dumfries.

Mackie, Professor J. D., C.B.E., M.A. (*Chairman of Council*), The University, Glasgow.

Mackie, Kenneth W., Glen Lyn, Salisbury Green, Southampton.

Mackie, Robert L., M.A., B.Litt., Abercraig, West Newport, Dundee.

Mackinnon, Rev. Donald, F.C. Manse, Kennoway, Fife.

Maclean, The Very Rev. Norman, D.D., Portree House, Portree, Skye.

MacLehose, Mrs. James, 5 Heriot Row, Edinburgh.

160 Macmillan, The Lord, G.C.V.O., LL.D., Moon Hall, Ewhurst, near Guildford, Surrey.

McNaughton, Duncan, M.A., F.S.A.Scot., West Grange, Culross, Fife.

Macpherson, Bruce W., Barrister-at-Law, Crogga, Port Soderick, Isle of Man.

Macpherson, James, Solicitor, Corn Exchange Road, Stirling.

Macrae, C., D.Phil., Auchraig, Barnton, Edinburgh.

Malcolm, Charles A., Ph.D., Signet Library, Edinburgh.

Mar and Kellie, The Earl of, K.T., Alloa House, Alloa.

Marshall, Charles Hay, S.S.C., 97 Seagate, Dundee.

Marshall, David C., Kilbucho Place, Broughton, Peebles-shire.

Marshall, Sir W. M., Solicitor, 3 Merry Street, Motherwell.

170 Mason, John, School House, South Queensferry, West Lothian.

Meikle, H. W., C.B.E., LL.D., D.Litt., 23 Riselaw Road, Edinburgh.

Meldrum, Rev. Neil, B.D., 26 Carden Place, Aberdeen.

Menzies, W., 6 St. Vincent Street, Edinburgh.

Michie, J. T., Windyknowe, Dunblane.

Mill, William, 109 Princes Street, Edinburgh.

Millar, Hugo B., c/o R. D. Millar & Co., 73 Robertson Street, Glasgow, C. 2.

Millar, Oliver, Tewes, Little Sampford, near Saffron Walden, Essex.

Miller, R. Pairman, S.S.C., 13 Heriot Row, Edinburgh.

Milne, Miss Isabel J., 87 Comiston Drive, Edinburgh.

180 Milne, James Fairweather, Rocksley House, Boddam, Peterhead.

Moncreiffe, Captain Iain, Scots Guards, House of Moncreiffe, Bridge of Earn.

Mooney, John, Cromwell Cottage, Kirkwall, Orkney.

Morison, H. P., Shawpark, Selkirk.

Muirhead, Roland E., Meikle Cloak, Lochwinnoch.

Murchison, Rev. T. M., M.A., 14 Kinross Avenue, Glasgow.

Nicholas, Don. L., Gatehampton Manor, Goring-on-Thames, Oxon.

Nicoll, A., 23 Rothesay Terrace, Edinburgh.

Oliver, Mrs. F. S., Edgerston, Jedburgh.

Oliver, J. W., D.Litt., 41 Barnton Terrace, Edinburgh.

190 Orr, John, 8 Coltbridge Gardens, Edinburgh.

Paton, Henry M., 5 Little Road, Liberton, Edinburgh.

Petrie, James A., ' Ashfield,' 7 Bonnington Grove, Edinburgh, 6.

Philip, Sheriff J. R., O.B.E., K.C., 53 Great King Street, Edinburgh.

Pirie-Gordon, of Buthlaw, Harry, D.S.C., F.S.A., Polesacre, Lowfield Heath, Crawley, Sussex.

Pollok, Mrs. Gladys M., Ronachan, Clachan, Tarbert, Argyll.

Porcelli, Lt.-Colonel The Baron, 56 South Street, Park Lane, London, W. 1.

Powrie, Thomas, 165A Brookside Lane, Walton, Stone, Staffs.

Prain, A. M., Advocate, Castellar, Crieff, Perthshire.

Pryde, G. S., Ph.D., 9 Great Western Terrace, Glasgow, W. 2.

200 Ramsay, Miss E. Lucy, Stainrigg, Coldstream.

Ramsay, Captain Iain, Junior Carlton Club, Pall Mall, London.

Reid, James A., 28 Anderson Street, Airdrie.

Reid, R. C., Cleuchbrae Cottage, Ruthwell, R.S.O., Dumfriesshire.

Reid, W. Stanford, Department of History, McGill University, Montreal, Canada.

Robb, James, B.D., LL.D., 26 Ormidale Terrace, Edinburgh.

Robertson, Ian Macdonald, LL.B., Advocate, 49 Moray Place, Edinburgh.

Rosebery, The Earl of, D.S.O., Dalmeny House, Edinburgh.

Ross, James, 10 Midmar Gardens, Edinburgh.

Rothwell, R. Norris, Baddeley Mount, Bowness-on-Windermere.

210 Russell, John, 4 Dudley Gardens, Leith, Edinburgh.

Salvesen, I. R. S., Bonnington House, Kirknewton, Midlothian.

Sanderson, Miss Elizabeth M. C., 8 East Fettes Avenue, Edinburgh.

Saunders, William, 15 Morningside Grove, Edinburgh.

Scott, David, Glenaros, Isle of Mull, by Oban.

Scott, Hon. Grizel Hepburne, Balfour Hostel, East Suffolk Road, Edinburgh.

Scott, R. Lyon, Braeside, Loanhead, Midlothian.

Shaw, Duncan, 6 Ulster Crescent, Edinburgh.

Simpson, W. Douglas, D.Litt., The University, Aberdeen.

Simson, Mrs. Annie, Balmanno, Laurencekirk, Kincardineshire.

220 Sinclair, The Rt. Hon. Sir Archibald, Bart., Thurso Castle, Caithness.

Smith, D. Baird, C.B.E., LL.D., 5 Kirklee Terrace, Glasgow, W. 2.

Smith, Miss Dorothea Nimmo, 19 Moray Place, Edinburgh.

Smith, Lt.-Col. Ian M., D.S.O., M.C., c/o The British Linen Bank, 38 Threadneedle Street, London, E.C. 2.

Smith, John, Birkhill, Coalburn, Lanarkshire.

Somerville, John, Solicitor, 9 Hermitage Terrace, Edinburgh.

Stair, The Earl of, D.S.O., Lochinch Castle, Stranraer, Wigtownshire.

Stark, William McNab, 58 North Court Street, Dundee.

Stenhouse, B. A., 11 Learmonth Park, Edinburgh.

Stevenson, Professor W. B., 31 Mansionhouse Road, Edinburgh.

230 Stewart, James, of Keil, Appin, Marlborough, Salisbury, Southern Rhodesia.

Stewart, Miss Helen C., 35 Wilton Place, London, S.W.

Stirling, Matthew, 49 Smith Street, London, S.W. 3.

Stodart, Charles, of Leaston, Humbie.

Strathie, A. C., Bemersyde, Kilmacolm, Renfrewshire.

Struthers, Major J. G., Armaddy Castle, by Oban, Argyll.

Swinton, Rev. Alan E., of Swinton House, Duns.

TAYLER, Miss HENRIETTA, Duff House, Arundel.

Thoms, David B., Strathview, Trinity Road, Brechin, Angus.

Thomson, Alexander, LL.B., 11 Moray Place, Edinburgh.

240 Thomson, David C., Inveravon, Broughty Ferry.

Thomson, J. Albert, c/o Brown Brothers Ltd., 26 Gt. Eastern Street, London.

Thomson, J. A., The Elms, Annan.

Thomson, Miss Mairi, 5 Abercorn Terrace, Edinburgh.

Thomson, Brig.-Gen. N. A., C.M.G., D.S.O. (retired), Mansfield, Kohstad, East Griqualand, South Africa.

Tod, Henry, W.S., 45 North Castle Street, Edinburgh.

URQUHART, DONALD, Bellair, Durban, Natal, South Africa.

WATERSTON, ROBERT, 27 Inverleith Terrace, Edinburgh.

Watson, Arthur, 23 Danes Drive, Scotstoun, Glasgow.

Watson, Professor James A. S., B.Sc., 4 Sheldon Avenue, Highgate, London.

250 Watt, Mrs. James, 7B Blackford Road, Edinburgh.

Watt, The Very Rev. Lauchlan Maclean, D.D., LL.D., Kinloch, Lochcarron, Ross-shire.

Weir, John L., 9 Frankfort Street, Glasgow, S. 1.

Whyte, Robert D., 33 Mountstuart Road, Rothesay.

Williamson, Peter, 45 Willowbrae Avenue, Edinburgh.

Wilson, Sir Garnet, LL.D., St. Colmes, 496 Perth Road, Dundee.

Wordie, William, 31 Kingsborough Gardens, Glasgow, W.2.

Wotherspoon, Robert, Solicitor, Inverness.

Wright, James M. B., of Auchinellan, Ford, Argyll.

Wyllie, Matthew, 169 West George Street, Glasgow, C. 2.

260 YOUNG, DAVID R., Solicitor, Kinross.

Young, James, Pitronan, Bonhard Road, Scone, Perth.

Young, Kenneth G., M.A., LL.B., W.S., Lindores, Muthill.

LIST OF LIBRARIES SUBSCRIBING

Aberdeen Public Library.
Aberdeen University Library.
Arbroath Public Library.
Ayr, Carnegie Public Library.
Baltimore, Peabody Institute, U.S.A.
Bearsden, by Glasgow, St. Peter's College.
Belfast Library and Society for Promoting Knowledge,
    Donegall Square North, Belfast (Linenhall Library).
Belfast, Queen's University.
Birmingham Public Libraries (Ref. Dept.).
10 Birmingham University Library.
Boston Athenæum, Mass., U.S.A.
Boston Public Library, Mass., U.S.A.
Bowdoin College Library, Brunswick, Maine, U.S.A.
Bristol University, Bristol.
Brussels, Bibliothèque Royale de Belgique, Belgium.
California University Library, U.S.A.
Cambridge University Library.
Canberra, Commonwealth National Library, Australia.
Cardiff Free Public Library.
20 Chicago, Newberry Library, U.S.A.
Chicago University Library, U.S.A.
Cincinnati, The General Library, University of Cincinnati,
    Ohio, U.S.A.
Cleveland Public Library, 325 Superior Avenue, N.W.,
    Cleveland, Ohio, U.S.A.
Coatbridge, Carnegie Public Library.
Columbia University Library, New York, U.S.A.
Copenhagen, Royal Library, Denmark.
Cornell University, Ithaca, New York, U.S.A.
Dartmouth College Library, Hanover, N.H., U.S.A.
Duke University Library, Durham, North Carolina, U.S.A.
30 Dumbarton, Free Public Library.
Dundee Public Library.
Dundee University College Library.
Dunfermline Public Library.
Dunfermline, Scottish Central Library for Students.
Dunoon, The Tulloch Free Library, Castle House.
Edinburgh, Church of Scotland Library.
Edinburgh, Corporation of the City of, City Chambers.

Edinburgh, Episcopal Church Theological Library, Coates Hall, Rosebery Crescent.

Edinburgh, Fraser Chair of Scottish History, Edinburgh University.

40 Edinburgh, Free Church Library, Bank Street.

Edinburgh, H.M. General Register House (Historical Department).

Edinburgh, Hope Trust, 31 Moray Place.

Edinburgh, New Club, Princes Street.

Edinburgh, New College Library, Assembly Hall, Mound.

Edinburgh, Protestant Institute of Scotland, 17 George IV. Bridge.

Edinburgh Public Library, George IV. Bridge.

Edinburgh, Royal College of Physicians, 9 Queen Street.

Edinburgh, St. Mary's Cathedral Library.

Edinburgh, Signet Library, Parliament Square.

50 Edinburgh, Society of Scottish Antiquaries, National Museum of Antiquities, Queen Street.

Edinburgh, Society of Solicitors before the Supreme Court.

Edinburgh, Speculative Society, University Buildings.

Edinburgh, The Stewart Society, 50 Melville Street.

Edinburgh University Library.

Falkirk Public Library.

Fort Augustus, St. Benedict's Abbey.

Fort William, West Highland Museum.

Glasgow, Baillie's Institution Free Library.

Glasgow, Faculty of Procurators.

60 Glasgow, Mitchell Library. (The Moir Fund.)

Glasgow University Library.

Glasgow Western Club.

Göteborg City and University Library, Sweden.

Harvard College Library, Cambridge, Mass., U.S.A.

Illinois University Library, Urbana, Ill., U.S.A.

Indiana, University of Notre Dame, U.S.A.

Inverness Public Library.

Iowa State University, Iowa, U.S.A.

Ireland, National Library of, Dublin.

70 Kilmarnock Public Library.

Leeds Library, Commercial Street, Leeds.

Leeds University, Brotherton Library.

Liverpool Public Library.

Liverpool University.

London, Antiquaries, Society of, Burlington House, Piccadilly, London, W. 1.

London, Corporation Library, Guildhall.

London, Institute of Historical Research, Malet Street, W.C. 1.

London Library, St. James's Square.

London, Public Record Office.

80 London, Reform Club, Pall Mall, S.W.

London, Royal Institution, W.

London School of Economics and Political Science, Houghton Street, Aldwych, London, W.C. 2.

London University, South Kensington, S.W.

London, University College, Gower Street, London.

Los Angeles Public Library, California, U.S.A.

Los Angeles, University of California Library, U.S.A.

Lund, Universitets Bibliotheket, Sweden.

Clan Mackay Society, Edinburgh.

Manchester, John Rylands Library.

90 Manchester Public Library.

Manchester University Library.

Melbourne, University of, Carlton, Australia.

Michigan, University of, General Library, Ann Arbor, Mich., U.S.A.

Minnesota, Library of University of Minneapolis, U.S.A.

Montreal, McGill University, Redpath Library, Canada.

Nashville, Joint University Library, Tennessee, U.S.A.

Netherlands Royal Library, The Hague, Holland.

Newcastle-upon-Tyne Public Library.

New South Wales Library, Sydney, Australia.

100 New York Public Library, Albany, New York, U.S.A.

New York State Library, U.S.A.

New York University, Washington Square Library, U.S.A.

Northwestern University Library, Evanston, Illinois, U.S.A.

Nottingham, Free Public Library.

Oregon University Library, Eugene, Oregon, U.S.A.

Ottawa, Parliamentary Library, Canada.

Oxford, All Souls College.

Oxford, Bodleian Library.

Oxford, Worcester College.

110 Paisley, Philosophical Institution.

Paris, Bibliothèque Nationale, France.

Pennsylvania Historical Society, U.S.A.
Pennsylvania University Library, Philadelphia, U.S.A.
Perth, Sandeman Public Library.
Pittsburgh, The University Library, U.S.A.
Princeton Theological Seminary, New Jersey, U.S.A.
Princeton University Library, New Jersey, U.S.A.
Reading University Library.
Rochester University Library, New York, U.S.A.
120 St. Andrews Hay Fleming Library.
St. Andrews University Library.
San Francisco Public Library, Civic Center, California, U.S.A.
San Marino, Henry E. Huntington Library and Art Gallery, California, U.S.A.
Sheffield, Free Public Library.
Sheffield University Library.
Stanford University Library, California, U.S.A.
Stirling Public Library.
Stockholm, A.B. Nordiska Bokhandeln, Sweden.
Stockholm, Royal Library, Sweden.
130 Stonyhurst College, Blackburn, Lancashire.
Texas, University of, Austin, Texas, U.S.A.
Toronto Reference Library, Canada.
Toronto University Library, Canada.
Upsala, Royal University Library, Sweden.
Utrecht, Historisch Genootschap, Holland.
Vaticana Biblioteca Apostolica, Città del Vaticano, Italy.
Victoria Public Library, Melbourne, Australia.
Wales, National Library of, Aberystwyth.
Washington, Library of Congress, U.S.A.
140 Washington, University Library, Seattle, Washington, U.S.A.
Wellington, Victoria University College, New Zealand.
Wick, Carnegie Public Library.
Wigan, Free Public Library.
Wisconsin, University of, U.S.A.
Yale, University Library, U.S.A.

Copies of the Society's Publications are presented to the following Libraries :—

British Museum, London.
National Library of Scotland, Edinburgh.

Scottish History Society

THE EXECUTIVE
1949-1950

President.
Rt. Hon. LORD COOPER, LL.D., Lord Justice General.

Chairman of Council.
Professor W. CROFT DICKINSON, D.Lit.

Council.
HENRIETTA TAYLER.
JAMES FERGUSSON.
Professor J. D. MACKIE, C.B.E.
H. W. MEIKLE, C.B.E., LL.D., D.Litt.
Mrs. ANNIE I. DUNLOP, O.B.E., D.Litt.
H. M. PATON.
Rev. DONALD MACKINNON.
G. S. PRYDE, Ph.D.
R. L. MACKIE.
Rev. D. E. EASSON, Ph.D.
Sir T. INNES of Learney, K.C.V.O.
R. C. REID.

Corresponding Members of Council.
G. M. TREVELYAN, O.M., C.B.E., F.B.A., D.C.L., LL.D.,
Litt.D., Master of Trinity College, Cambridge.
Professor V. H. GALBRAITH, F.B.A., Regius Professor of Modern
History in the University of Oxford.
B. H. SUMNER, F.B.A., Warden of All Souls College, Oxford.

Hon. Treasurer.
J. DOUGLAS H. DICKSON, W.S., Mus.Doc.,
66 Queen Street, Edinburgh.

Hon. Secretary.
E. W. M. BALFOUR-MELVILLE, D.Litt., History Department,
The University, Edinburgh.

M

RULES

1. THE object of the Society is the discovery and printing, under selected editorship, of unpublished documents illustrative of the civil, religious, and social history of Scotland. The Society will also undertake, in exceptional cases, to issue translations of printed works of a similar nature which have not hitherto been accessible in English.

2. The affairs of the Society shall be managed by a Council, consisting of a Chairman, Treasurer, Secretary, and twelve elected Members, five to make a quorum. Three of the twelve elected Members shall retire annually by ballot, but they shall be eligible for re-election.

3. The Annual Subscription to the Society shall be One Guinea. The publications of the Society shall not be delivered to any Member whose Subscription is in arrear, and no Member shall be permitted to receive more than one copy of the Society's publications.

4. The Society will undertake the issue of its own publications, *i.e.* without the intervention of a publisher or any other paid agent.

5. The Society normally issues one volume each year.

6. An Annual General Meeting of the Society shall be held at the end of October, or at an approximate date to be determined by the Council.

7. Two stated Meetings of the Council shall be held each year, one on the last Tuesday of May, the other on the Tuesday preceding the day upon which the Annual General Meeting shall be held. The Secretary, on the request of three Members of the Council, shall call a special meeting of the Council.

8. Editors shall receive 20 copies of each volume they edit for the Society.

9. The owners of Manuscripts published by the Society will also be presented with a certain number of copies.

10. The Annual Balance-Sheet, Rules, and List of Members shall be printed.

11. No alteration shall be made in these Rules except at a General Meeting of the Society. A fortnight's notice of any alteration to be proposed shall be given to the Members of the Council.

PUBLICATIONS

OF THE

SCOTTISH HISTORY SOCIETY

For the year 1886-1887.

1. BISHOP POCOCKE'S TOURS IN SCOTLAND, 1747-1760. Edited by D. W. KEMP.

2. DIARY AND ACCOUNT BOOK OF WILLIAM CUNNINGHAM OF CRAIGENDS, 1673-1680. Edited by the Rev. JAMES DODDS, D.D.

For the year 1887-1888.

3. GRAMEIDOS LIBRI SEX : an heroic poem on the Campaign of 1689, by JAMES PHILIP of Almerieclose. Translated and edited by the Rev. A. D. MURDOCH.

4. THE REGISTER OF THE KIRK-SESSION OF ST. ANDREWS. Part I, 1559-1582. Edited by D. HAY FLEMING.

For the year 1888-1889.

5. DIARY OF THE REV. JOHN MILL, Minister in Shetland, 1740-1803. Edited by GILBERT GOUDIE.

6. NARRATIVE OF MR. JAMES NIMMO, A COVENANTER, 1654-1709. Edited by W. G. SCOTT-MONCRIEFF.

7. THE REGISTER OF THE KIRK-SESSION OF ST. ANDREWS. Part II, 1583-1600. Edited by D. HAY FLEMING.

For the year 1889-1890.

8. A LIST OF PERSONS CONCERNED IN THE REBELLION (1745). With a Preface by the EARL OF ROSEBERY.
   Presented to the Society by the Earl of Rosebery.

9. GLAMIS PAPERS : The 'BOOK OF RECORD,' a Diary written by PATRICK, FIRST EARL OF STRATHMORE, and other documents (1684-89). Edited by A. H. MILLAR.

10. JOHN MAJOR'S HISTORY OF GREATER BRITAIN (1521). Translated and edited by ARCHIBALD CONSTABLE.

For the year 1890-1891.

11. THE RECORDS OF THE COMMISSIONS OF THE GENERAL ASSEMBLIES, 1646-47. Edited by the Rev. Professor MITCHELL, D.D., and the Rev. JAMES CHRISTIE, D.D.

12. COURT-BOOK OF THE BARONY OF URIE, 1604-1747. Edited by the Rev. D. G. BARRON.

For the year 1891-1892.

13. MEMOIRS OF SIR JOHN CLERK OF PENICUIK, BARONET. Extracted by himself from his own Journals, 1676-1755. Edited by JOHN M. GRAY.

14. DIARY OF COL. THE HON. JOHN ERSKINE OF CARNOCK, 1683-1687. Edited by the Rev. WALTER MACLEOD.

For the year 1892-1893.

15. MISCELLANY OF THE SCOTTISH HISTORY SOCIETY. Vol. I.

16. ACCOUNT BOOK OF SIR JOHN FOULIS OF RAVELSTON (1671-1707). Edited by the Rev. A. W. CORNELIUS HALLEN.

For the year 1893-1894.

17. LETTERS AND PAPERS ILLUSTRATING THE RELATIONS BETWEEN CHARLES II AND SCOTLAND IN 1650. Edited by SAMUEL RAWSON GARDINER, D.C.L., etc.

18. SCOTLAND AND THE COMMONWEALTH. LETTERS AND PAPERS RELATING TO THE MILITARY GOVERNMENT OF SCOTLAND, Aug. 1651-Dec. 1653. Edited by C. H. FIRTH, M.A.

For the year 1894-1895.

19. THE JACOBITE ATTEMPT OF 1719. LETTERS OF JAMES, SECOND DUKE OF ORMONDE. Edited by W. K. DICKSON.

20, 21. THE LYON IN MOURNING, OR A COLLECTION OF SPEECHES, LETTERS, JOURNALS, ETC., RELATIVE TO THE AFFAIRS OF PRINCE CHARLES EDWARD STUART, by BISHOP FORBES. 1746-1775. Edited by HENRY PATON. Vols. I and II.

For the year 1895-1896.

22. THE LYON IN MOURNING. Vol. III.

23. ITINERARY OF PRINCE CHARLES EDWARD (Supplement to the Lyon in Mourning). Compiled by W. B. BLAIKIE.

24. EXTRACTS FROM THE PRESBYTERY RECORDS OF INVERNESS AND DINGWALL FROM 1638 TO 1688. Edited by WILLIAM MACKAY.

25. RECORDS OF THE COMMISSIONS OF THE GENERAL ASSEMBLIES (*continued*) for the years 1648 and 1649. Edited by the Rev. Professor MITCHELL, D.D., and Rev. JAMES CHRISTIE, D.D.

For the year 1896-1897.

26. WARISTON'S DIARY AND OTHER PAPERS—
JOHNSTON OF WARISTON'S DIARY, 1639. Edited by G. M.
PAUL.—THE HONOURS OF SCOTLAND, 1651-52. C. R. A.
HOWDEN.—THE EARL OF MAR'S LEGACIES, 1722, 1726.
Hon. S. ERSKINE.—LETTERS BY MRS. GRANT OF LAGGAN.
J. R. N. MACPHAIL.
Presented to the Society by Messrs. T. and A. Constable.

27. MEMORIALS OF JOHN MURRAY OF BROUGHTON, 1740-1747.
Edited by R. FITZROY BELL.

28. THE COMPT BUIK OF DAVID WEDDERBURNE, MERCHANT OF
DUNDEE, 1587-1630. Edited by A. H. MILLAR.

For the year 1897-1898.

29, 30. THE CORRESPONDENCE OF DE MONTEREUL AND THE
BROTHERS DE BELLIÈVRE, FRENCH AMBASSADORS IN
ENGLAND AND SCOTLAND, 1645-1648. Edited, with Trans-
lation, by J. G. FOTHERINGHAM. 2 vols.

For the year 1898-1899.

31. SCOTLAND AND THE PROTECTORATE. LETTERS AND PAPERS
RELATING TO THE MILITARY GOVERNMENT OF SCOTLAND,
FROM JANUARY 1654 TO JUNE 1659. Edited by C. H.
FIRTH, M.A.

32. PAPERS ILLUSTRATING THE HISTORY OF THE SCOTS BRIGADE
IN THE SERVICE OF THE UNITED NETHERLANDS. 1572-1782.
Edited by JAMES FERGUSON. Vol. I, 1572-1697.

33, 34. MACFARLANE'S GENEALOGICAL COLLECTIONS CON-
CERNING FAMILIES IN SCOTLAND ; Manuscripts in the
Advocates' Library. 2 vols. Edited by J. T. CLARK,
Keeper of the Library.
Presented to the Society by the Trustees of the late Sir William Fraser, K.C.B.

For the year 1899-1900.

35. PAPERS ON THE SCOTS BRIGADE IN HOLLAND, 1572-1782.
Edited by JAMES FERGUSON. Vol. II, 1698-1782.

36. JOURNAL OF A FOREIGN TOUR IN 1665 AND 1666, ETC., BY
SIR JOHN LAUDER, LORD FOUNTAINHALL. Edited by
DONALD CRAWFORD.

37. PAPAL NEGOTIATIONS WITH MARY QUEEN OF SCOTS DURING
HER REIGN IN SCOTLAND. Chiefly from the Vatican
Archives. Edited by the Rev. J. HUNGERFORD POLLEN,
S.J.

For the year 1900-1901.

38. PAPERS ON THE SCOTS BRIGADE IN HOLLAND, 1572-1782. Edited by JAMES FERGUSON. Vol. III.

39. THE DIARY OF ANDREW HAY OF CRAIGNETHAN, 1659-60. Edited by A. G. REID, F.S.A.Scot.

For the year 1901-1902.

40. NEGOTIATIONS FOR THE UNION OF ENGLAND AND SCOTLAND IN 1651-53. Edited by C. SANFORD TERRY.

41. THE LOYALL DISSUASIVE. Written in 1703 by Sir ÆNEAS MACPHERSON. Edited by the Rev. A. D. MURDOCH.

For the year 1902-1903.

42. THE CHARTULARY OF LINDORES, 1195-1479. Edited by the Right Rev. JOHN DOWDEN, D.D., Bishop of Edinburgh.

43. A LETTER FROM MARY QUEEN OF SCOTS TO THE DUKE OF GUISE, Jan. 1562. Reproduced in Facsimile. Edited by the Rev. J. HUNGERFORD POLLEN, S.J.
Presented to the Society by the family of the late Mr. Scott, of Halkshill.

44. MISCELLANY OF THE SCOTTISH HISTORY SOCIETY. Vol. II.

45. LETTERS OF JOHN COCKBURN OF ORMISTOUN TO HIS GARDENER, 1727-1743. Edited by JAMES COLVILLE, D.Sc.

For the year 1903-1904.

46. MINUTE BOOK OF THE MANAGERS OF THE NEW MILLS CLOTH MANUFACTORY, 1681-1690. Edited by W. R. SCOTT.

47. CHRONICLES OF THE FRASERS ; being the Wardlaw Manuscript entitled ' Polichronicon seu Policratica Temporum, or, the true Genealogy of the Frasers.' By Master JAMES FRASER. Edited by WILLIAM MACKAY.

48. PROCEEDINGS OF THE JUSTICIARY COURT FROM 1661 TO 1678. Vol. I, 1661-1669. Edited by Sheriff SCOTT-MONCRIEFF.

For the year 1904-1905.

49. PROCEEDINGS OF THE JUSTICIARY COURT FROM 1661 TO 1678. Vol. II, 1669-1678. Edited by Sheriff SCOTT-MONCRIEFF.

50. RECORDS OF THE BARON COURT OF STITCHILL, 1655-1807. Edited by CLEMENT B. GUNN, M.D., Peebles.

51. MACFARLANE'S GEOGRAPHICAL COLLECTIONS. Vol. I. Edited by Sir ARTHUR MITCHELL, K.C.B.

For the year 1905-1906.

52, 53. MACFARLANE'S GEOGRAPHICAL COLLECTIONS. Vols. II and III. Edited by Sir ARTHUR MITCHELL, K.C.B.

54. STATUTA ECCLESIÆ SCOTICANÆ, 1225-1559. Translated and edited by DAVID PATRICK, LL.D.

For the year 1906-1907.

55. THE HOUSE BOOKE OF ACCOMPS, OCHTERTYRE, 1737-39. Edited by JAMES COLVILLE, D.Sc.

56. THE CHARTERS OF THE ABBEY OF INCHAFFRAY. Edited by W. A. LINDSAY, K.C., the Right Rev. Bishop DOWDEN, D.D., and J. MAITLAND THOMSON, LL.D.

57. A SELECTION OF THE FORFEITED ESTATES PAPERS PRE-SERVED IN H.M. GENERAL REGISTER HOUSE AND ELSE-WHERE. Edited by A. H. MILLAR, LL.D.

For the year 1907-1908.

58. RECORDS OF THE COMMISSIONS OF THE GENERAL ASSEMB-LIES (*continued*), for the years 1650-52. Edited by the Rev. JAMES CHRISTIE, D.D.

59. PAPERS RELATING TO THE SCOTS IN POLAND. Edited by A. FRANCIS STEUART.

For the year 1908-1909.

60. SIR THOMAS CRAIG'S DE UNIONE REGNORUM BRITANNIÆ TRACTATUS. Edited, with an English Translation, by C. SANFORD TERRY.

61. JOHNSTON OF WARISTON'S MEMENTO QUAMDIU VIVAS, AND DIARY FROM 1632 to 1639. Edited by G. M. PAUL, LL.D., D.K.S.

SECOND SERIES.

For the year 1909-1910.

1. THE HOUSEHOLD BOOK OF LADY GRISELL BAILLIE, 1692-1733. Edited by R. SCOTT-MONCRIEFF, W.S.

2. ORIGINS OF THE '45 AND OTHER NARRATIVES. Edited by W. B. BLAIKIE, LL.D.

3. CORRESPONDENCE OF JAMES, FOURTH EARL OF FINDLATER AND FIRST EARL OF SEAFIELD, LORD CHANCELLOR OF SCOTLAND. Edited by JAMES GRANT, M.A., LL.B.

For the year 1910-1911.

4. RENTALE SANCTI ANDREE; BEING CHAMBERLAIN AND GRANITAR ACCOUNTS OF THE ARCHBISHOPRIC IN THE TIME OF CARDINAL BETOUN, 1538-1546. Translated and edited by ROBERT KERR HANNAY.

5. HIGHLAND PAPERS. Vol. I. Edited by J. R. N. MACPHAIL, K.C.

For the year 1911-1912.

6. SELECTIONS FROM THE RECORDS OF THE REGALITY OF MELROSE. Vol. I. Edited by C. S. ROMANES, C.A.

7. RECORDS OF THE EARLDOM OF ORKNEY. Edited by J. S. CLOUSTON.

For the year 1912-1913.

8. SELECTIONS FROM THE RECORDS OF THE REGALITY OF MELROSE. Vol. II. Edited by C. S. ROMANES, C.A.

9. SELECTIONS FROM THE LETTER BOOKS OF JOHN STEUART, BAILIE OF INVERNESS. Edited by WILLIAM MACKAY, LL.D.

For the year 1913-1914.

10. RENTALE DUNKELDENSE; BEING THE ACCOUNTS OF THE CHAMBERLAIN OF THE BISHOPRIC OF DUNKELD, A.D. 1506-1517. Edited by R. K. HANNAY.

11. LETTERS OF THE EARL OF SEAFIELD AND OTHERS, ILLUSTRATIVE OF THE HISTORY OF SCOTLAND DURING THE REIGN OF QUEEN ANNE. Edited by Professor HUME BROWN.

For the year 1914-1915.

12. HIGHLAND PAPERS. Vol. II. Edited by J. R. N. MACPHAIL, K.C. (March 1916.)
  (*Note.*—ORIGINS OF THE '45, issued for 1909-1910, is issued also for 1914-1915.)

For the year 1915-1916.

13. SELECTIONS FROM THE RECORDS OF THE REGALITY OF MELROSE. Vol. III. Edited by C. S. ROMANES, C.A. (February 1917.)

14. A CONTRIBUTION TO THE BIBLIOGRAPHY OF SCOTTISH TOPOGRAPHY. Edited by the late Sir ARTHUR MITCHELL and C. G. CASH. Vol. I. (March 1917.)

For the year 1916-1917.

15. BIBLIOGRAPHY OF SCOTTISH TOPOGRAPHY. Vol. II.
(May 1917.)

16. PAPERS RELATING TO THE ARMY OF THE SOLEMN LEAGUE
AND COVENANT, 1643-1647. Vol. I. Edited by Professor
C. SANFORD TERRY. (October 1917.)

For the year 1917-1918.

17. PAPERS RELATING TO THE ARMY OF THE SOLEMN LEAGUE
AND COVENANT, 1643-1647. Vol. II. (December 1917.)

18. WARISTON'S DIARY. Vol. II. Edited by D. HAY FLEMING,
LL.D. (February 1919.)

For the year 1918-1919.

19. MISCELLANY OF THE SCOTTISH HISTORY SOCIETY. Vol. III.

20. HIGHLAND PAPERS. Vol. III. Edited by J. R. N.
MACPHAIL, K.C.

THIRD SERIES.

For the year 1919-1920.

1. REGISTER OF THE CONSULTATIONS OF THE MINISTERS OF
EDINBURGH. Vol. I. 1652-1657. Edited by the Rev.
W. STEPHEN, B.D.

For the year 1920-1921.

2. DIARY OF GEORGE RIDPATH, MINISTER OF STITCHEL, 1755-
1761. Edited by Sir JAMES BALFOUR PAUL, C.V.O., LL.D.

For the year 1921-1922.

3. THE CONFESSIONS OF BABINGTON AND OTHER PAPERS
RELATING TO THE LAST DAYS OF MARY QUEEN OF SCOTS.
Edited by the Rev. J. H. POLLEN, S.J.

For the year 1922-1923.

4. FOREIGN CORRESPONDENCE WITH MARIE DE LORRAINE,
QUEEN OF SCOTLAND (BALCARRES PAPERS), 1537-1548.
Vol. I. Edited by MARGUERITE WOOD, M.A.

5. SELECTION FROM THE PAPERS OF THE LATE SIR WILLIAM
FRASER, K.C.B. Edited by J. R. N. MACPHAIL, K.C.
Presented to the Society by the Trustees of the late Sir William Fraser, K.C.B.

For the year 1923-1924.

6. PAPERS RELATING TO THE SHIPS AND VOYAGES OF THE COMPANY OF SCOTLAND TRADING TO AFRICA AND THE INDIES, 1696-1707. Edited by GEORGE P. INSH, D.Litt.

For the year 1924-1925.

7. FOREIGN CORRESPONDENCE WITH MARIE DE LORRAINE, QUEEN OF SCOTLAND (BALCARRES PAPERS), 1548-1557. Vol. II. Edited by MARGUERITE WOOD, M.A.

For the year 1925-1926.

8. THE EARLY RECORDS OF THE UNIVERSITY OF ST. ANDREWS, 1413-1579. Edited by J. MAITLAND ANDERSON, LL.D.

9. MISCELLANY OF THE SCOTTISH HISTORY SOCIETY. Vol. IV. CORDARA'S COMMENTARY ON THE EXPEDITION TO SCOTLAND MADE BY CHARLES EDWARD STUART, PRINCE OF WALES. Edited by Sir BRUCE SETON, C.B.—THE CRAIGNISH MS. Edited by HERBERT CAMPBELL.—MISCELLANEOUS CHARTERS, 1165-1300, FROM TRANSCRIPTS IN THE COLLECTION OF THE LATE SIR WILLIAM FRASER, K.C.B. Edited by WILLIAM ANGUS.

For the year 1926-1927.

10. THE SCOTTISH CORRESPONDENCE OF MARY OF LORRAINE, 1543-1560. Edited by ANNIE I. CAMERON, M.A., Ph.D.

11. JOURNAL OF THOMAS CUNINGHAM, 1640-1654, CONSERVATOR AT CAMPVERE. Edited by ELINOR JOAN COURTHOPE, M.A.

For the year 1927-1928.

12. THE SHERIFF COURT BOOK OF FIFE, 1515-1522. Edited by WILLIAM CROFT DICKINSON, M.A., Ph.D.

13. THE PRISONERS OF THE '45. Vol. I. Edited by Sir BRUCE SETON, Bart. of Abercorn, C.B., and Mrs. JEAN GORDON ARNOT.

For the year 1928-1929.

14, 15. THE PRISONERS OF THE '45. Vols. II and III.

For the year 1929-1930.

16. REGISTER OF THE CONSULTATIONS OF THE MINISTERS OF EDINBURGH. Vol. II, 1657-1660. Edited by the Rev. W. STEPHEN, B.D.

17. THE MINUTES OF THE JUSTICES OF THE PEACE FOR LANARKSHIRE, 1707-1723. Edited by C. A. MALCOLM, M.A., Ph.D.
(October 1931.)

For the year 1930-1931.

18. THE WARRENDER PAPERS. Vol. I, 1301-1587. Edited by ANNIE I. CAMERON, M.A., Ph.D., with Introduction by Principal ROBERT S. RAIT, C.B.E., LL.D.

For the year 1931-1932.

19. THE WARRENDER PAPERS. Vol. II, 1587-1603. Edited by ANNIE I. CAMERON, M.A., Ph.D., with Introduction by Principal ROBERT S. RAIT, C.B.E., LL.D.

20. FLODDEN PAPERS. Edited by MARGUERITE WOOD, Ph.D.

For the year 1932-1933.

21. MISCELLANY OF THE SCOTTISH HISTORY SOCIETY. Vol. V. FRASER CHARTERS. Edited by WILLIAM ANGUS.—BAGIMOND'S ROLL FOR THE ARCHDEACONRY OF TEVIOTDALE. Edited by ANNIE I. CAMERON.—LAUDERDALE CORRESPONDENCE. Edited by HENRY M. PATON.—LETTERS OF ALEXANDER MONRO. Edited by WILLIAM KIRK DICKSON. —JACOBITE PAPERS AT AVIGNON. Edited by HENRIETTA TAYLER.—MARCHMONT CORRESPONDENCE RELATING TO THE '45. Edited by the Hon. G. F. C. HEPBURNE-SCOTT.— AUTOBIOGRAPHY OF EARL MARISCHAL KEITH. Edited by J. Y. T. GREIG.

22. HIGHLAND PAPERS. Vol. IV. Edited by J. R. N. MACPHAIL, K.C., with Biographical Introduction by WILLIAM K. DICKSON, LL.D.

For the year 1933-1934.

23. CALENDAR OF SCOTTISH SUPPLICATIONS TO ROME, 1418-1422. Edited by the Rev. and Hon. E. R. LINDSAY, M.A., and ANNIE I. CAMERON, M.A., D.Litt.

24. EARLY CORRESPONDENCE OF ROBERT WODROW. Edited by L. W. SHARP, M.A., Ph.D. (December 1937.)

For the year 1934-1935.

25. WARRENDER LETTERS. CORRESPONDENCE OF SIR GEORGE WARRENDER, LORD PROVOST OF EDINBURGH, 1715. Edited by WILLIAM K. DICKSON, LL.D.

26. COMMENTARY ON THE RULE OF ST. AUGUSTINE BY ROBERTUS RICHARDINUS. Edited by G. G. COULTON, Litt.D., D.Lit., F.B.A.

For the year 1935-1936.

27. SURVEY OF LOCHTAYSIDE, 1769. Edited by MARGARET M. McARTHUR, M.A., LL.B.

28. AYR BURGH ACCOUNTS, 1534-1624. Edited by G. S. PRYDE, M.A., Ph.D.

For the year 1936-1937.

29. BARONY COURT BOOK OF CARNWATH, 1523-1542. Edited by W. C. DICKINSON, D.Lit.

30. CHRONICLE OF HOLYROOD. Edited by MARJORIE OGILVIE ANDERSON, B.A., with some additional notes by ALAN ORR ANDERSON, LL.D.

For the year 1937-1938.

31. THE JACOBITE COURT AT ROME, 1719. Edited by HENRIETTA TAYLER.

32. INCHCOLM CHARTERS. Edited by Rev. D. E. EASSON, B.D., Ph.D., and ANGUS MACDONALD, M.A., Ph.D.

For the year 1938-1939.

33. MISCELLANY OF THE SCOTTISH HISTORY SOCIETY. Vol. VI. BAGIMOND'S ROLL. Edited by ANNIE I. DUNLOP, D.Litt.— FOUNDATION-CHARTER OF THE COLLEGIATE CHURCH OF DUNBAR. Edited by D. E. EASSON, Ph.D.—LETTERS FROM JOHN, SECOND EARL OF LAUDERDALE, TO JOHN, SECOND EARL OF TWEEDDALE, AND OTHERS. Edited by HENRY M. PATON.—MEMORIES OF AYRSHIRE ABOUT 1780 BY THE REV. JOHN MITCHELL, D.D. Edited by WILLIAM KIRK DICKSON.

34. WARISTON'S DIARY. Vol. III. Edited by J. D. OGILVIE.

For the year 1939-1940.

35. MISCELLANY OF THE SCOTTISH HISTORY SOCIETY. Vol. VII. DIARY OF SIR WILLIAM DRUMMOND OF HAWTHORNDEN, 1657-1659. Edited by H. W. MEIKLE, D.Litt.—THE EXILED STEWARTS IN ITALY. Edited by HELEN C. STEWART.—THE LOCHARKAIG TREASURE. Edited by MARION F. HAMILTON.

For the year 1940-1941.

36. TWO MISSIONS OF JACQUES DE LA BROSSE, 1543 AND 1560. Edited by G. DICKINSON.

For the year 1941-1942.

37. MINUTES OF THE SYNOD OF ARGYLL, 1639-1651. Edited by DUNCAN C. MACTAVISH.

For the year 1942-1943.

38. MINUTES OF THE SYNOD OF ARGYLL, 1652-1661. Edited by DUNCAN C. MACTAVISH, with Introduction by J. D. OGILVIE.

For the year 1943-1944.

39. MONYMUSK PAPERS. Edited by HENRY HAMILTON, D.Litt.

For the year 1944-1945.

40. CHARTERS OF THE ABBEY OF COUPAR ANGUS. Vol. I. Edited by D. E. EASSON, Ph.D.

For the year 1945-1946.

41. CHARTERS OF THE ABBEY OF COUPAR ANGUS. Vol. II. Edited by D. E. EASSON, Ph.D.

For the years 1946-1947 *and* 1947-1948.

42. ACCOUNTS OF THE COLLECTORS OF THE THIRDS OF BENE-FICES, 1561-1572. Edited by GORDON DONALDSON, Ph.D.

For the year 1948-1949.

43. MISCELLANY OF THE SCOTTISH HISTORY SOCIETY. Vol. VIII. MISCELLANEOUS MONASTIC CHARTERS. Edited by D. E. EASSON, Ph.D.—A LETTER OF JAMES III TO CHARLES, DUKE OF BURGUNDY. Edited by C. A. J. ARMSTRONG.— THE ENGLISH ARMY AT FLODDEN. Edited by J. D. MACKIE, LL.D.—LORD CHANCELLOR GLAMIS AND THEODORE BEZA. Edited by GORDON DONALDSON, Ph.D.—A GRANDSON OF PRINCE CHARLES EDWARD STEWART. Edited by HENRIETTA TAYLER.—A RENFREWSHIRE FARM, 1822-1830. Edited by G. S. PRYDE, Ph.D.

44. SCOTTISH POPULATION STATISTICS. Edited by J. G. KYD.

In preparation.

1. CALENDAR OF LETTERS OF JAMES IV. Edited by R. K. HANNAY, LL.D., and R. L. MACKIE.

2. ABERDEEN BURGH COURT RECORDS. Edited by W. CROFT DICKINSON, D.Lit.

3. KIRKINTILLOCH BURGH COURT BOOK. Edited by G. S. PRYDE, Ph.D.

4. CORRESPONDENCE OF JAMES II, KING OF SCOTS, WITH CHARLES VII, KING OF FRANCE. Edited by ANNIE I. DUNLOP, D.Litt.

5. ACCOUNT OF THE PROCEEDINGS OF THE MEETING OF THE ESTATES IN SCOTLAND, 1689-1690. Edited by E. W. M. BALFOUR-MELVILLE, D.Litt.